Doing Business in Kenya

A deep dive into a success story in African business development, this book provides a multi-layered perspective on the realities of doing business in Kenya.

The book's detailed information about the economic, social, technological, and cultural dimensions of Kenyan society enables a greater understanding of the major issues affecting business development, and actionable recommendations clarify the possible paths to starting and developing a business venture in Kenya. Given Africa's heterogeneity, it cannot be perfectly represented by one country. Still, Kenya closely mirrors Africa's major economic trends and cultural values: understanding Kenya's business landscape provides invaluable skills to do business throughout Africa.

Businesspeople, policymakers, investors, students, and scholars will value this book's in-depth first-hand knowledge to help them make informed decisions about doing business in Africa or Kenya specifically.

Dr. Wakiuru Wamwara, Ph.D., is a Professor of Marketing at the Raj Soin College of Business and Economics at Wright State University. Dr. Wamwara's research has been published in the Journal of Business Research, Journal of Consumer Behaviour, Event Management Journal, and Journal of Immigrant and Refugee Studies, among others. Dr. Wamwara was a Carnegie Africa Diaspora Fellow at Africa Nazarene University and KCA University and is on the Fulbright Specialist roster as an African Region Specialist.

John E. Spillan, Ph.D., is a Professor of Management in the Thomas School of Business at The University of North Carolina At Pembroke. His research interests center on International Business with a specific interest in Latin America and Eastern Europe. His articles and books have appeared in the International Journal of Logistics Management, Business Logistics, Latin American Business Review, Journal of World Business, and Journal of Small Business Strategy. He has authored six books, 4 of them focused on business in Latin America.

Charles M. Onchoke, DBA, LL.B, Masters in Accounting and Finance, is a public financial management expert with several years of experience in Kenya and the USA. In 2022, he was elected member of Parliament for the Bonchari constituency. Previously, Dr. Onchoke served as the Director of Finance at the National Treasury of Kenya. Dr. Onchoke served on the boards of Kenya Roads Board, the National Government Constituencies Development Fund, and New KCC Ltd. Dr. Onchoke worked as the Business Manager of the Medical School at Texas Tech University. Dr. Onchoke served as treasurer of the city of Kisumu and deputy city treasurer of the city of Nairobi. He is an advocate of the High Court of Kenya.

Doing Business in Kenya

Opportunities and Challenges

**Wakiuru Wamwara,
John E. Spillan, and
Charles M. Onchoke**

Routledge
Taylor & Francis Group

NEW YORK AND LONDON

Designed cover image: Evans Amwanzo

First published 2023
by Routledge
605 Third Avenue, New York, NY 10158

and by Routledge
4 Park Square, Milton Park, Abingdon, Oxon, OX14 4RN

Routledge is an imprint of the Taylor & Francis Group, an Informa business

ISBN: 978-0-367-55791-1 (hbk)
ISBN: 978-0-367-55766-9 (pbk)
ISBN: 978-1-003-09515-6 (ebk)

DOI: 10.4324/9781003095156

Typeset in Bembo
by MPS Limited, Dehradun

For My daughters Aziza Wanjiru and Habiba Nyambura for their encouragement, love, and support. You are always my motivation!

Wakiuru Wamwara

For My Dear Wife, Martha, who has listened to my words and always has a solution to my problems. She has been my mainstay, especially while writing this important book. Thanks for your dedication, love, and patience.

John E. Spillan

For my family, none of this would have been possible without your love and support.

Charles M. Onchoke

Contents

About the Authors

Dr. Wakiuru Wamwara, Ph.D., is a Professor of Marketing at the Raj Soin College of Business and Economics at Wright State University. Her research interests center on international marketing, cross-cultural consumer behavior, and immigrant acculturation. Dr. Wamwara's research has been published in the Journal of African Interdisciplinary Studies, Journal of Business Research, Journal of Consumer Behavior, Event Management Journal, Advances in Consumer Research, Journal of Immigrant and Refugee Studies, and African Journal of Business Management, among others. Dr. Wamwara was a Carnegie Africa Diaspora Fellow at Africa Nazarene University and KCA University. She has delivered Kenya note speeches at the AIBUMA conference (University of Nairobi) and the AISA International Interdisciplinary Conference (Multimedia University of Kenya). She has lectured worldwide on semesters at sea and in Finland, Germany, and Kenya. Dr. Wamwara is on the Fulbright Specialist roster as an African Region Specialist for 3 years ending in 2022. She served as treasurer of the Kenya Studies and Scholars Association (KESSA) and serves on the board of the Kenya USA Diaspora Sacco. Before working in academia, she worked for the Kenyan government, the Kenya Association of Manufacturers, and the United Nations Human Settlements Programme (UN-HABITAT).

John E. Spillan, Ph.D., serves as Professor of Management and Director of International Affairs in the School of Business at The University of North Carolina At Pembroke. His research interests center on International Business with a specific interest in Latin America and Eastern Europe. His articles and books have appeared in the International Journal of Logistics Management, Business Logistics, Latin American Business Review, Journal of World Business, Journal of East-West Business, Journal of Teaching in International Business, Chinese Management Studies, Journal of Small Business Strategy, Journal of World Business, International Journal of Logistic Management, Journal of Transportation Management, Journal of Small Business Management, Journal of Global Marketing. He has authored six books, 4 of them focused on business in Latin America. He has traveled in Europe, Latin America, China, and Africa.

Charles M. Onchoke, DBA, LLB, Masters in Accounting and Finance, is a public financial management expert with several years of experience in Kenya and the USA. In 2022, he was elected member of Parliament for the Bonchari constituency. Previously, Dr. Onchoke served as the Director of Finance at the National Treasury of Kenya. Dr. Onchoke served on the boards of Kenya Roads Board, the National Government Constituencies Development Fund, and New KCC Ltd. Dr. Onchoke worked as the Business Manager of the Medical School at Texas Tech University. Dr. Onchoke served as treasurer of the city of Kisumu and deputy city treasurer of the city of Nairobi. He is an advocate of the High Court of Kenya.

Acknowledgments

The authors would like to thank the following: Professor Geoffrey M. Muluvi (Vice-Chancellor, SEKU) and Mr. Nicholas Mwanzia (Quality Control Manager – Kicotec), Dr. Kimani Gicuhi (African Nazarene University), Mr. Steve Chege (CEO Café Ngoma), and Mr. Stephen Githiga (CEO The Fresh Products), Jennifer Barassa (CEO Top Image Africa), Mr. Wilfred Mose (CEO The Ruby Group), Ms. Olivia Rachier (Managing Director Kenya Investment Authority, KIA), Garachi Adi and Pius Rotich both of (KIA) for all of their assistance during the data collection phase of this work. We are grateful for the individual part that each of you played in ensuring that we had the most current and relevant information. A special thank you to Kicotec and Fresh Products for facilitating visits to the Kitui manufacturing plant and the Fresh Products packhouse in Thika.

The authors would also like to thank our book editors, Meredith Norwich and Bethany Nelson at Taylor Francis, for their hard work that greatly improved this book.

The second author would like to acknowledge Dr. Edwin Mensah of Ghana. The latter initially sparked his interest in studying African businesses and encouraged him to pursue more in-depth research in other parts of Africa.

A special thank you to the Rike Consumer Research Fund at Wright State University for funding this research. Additionally, the first author would like to thank Professor Kendall Goodrich (Marketing Department Chair) for his unwavering support of all of her international educational endeavors.

1 Introduction to Kenya

1.1 Overview

This chapter presents an overview of Kenya's location, its regional positioning, business operations and opportunities, the investment climate and the structure of the book. This is followed by the rationale and timeliness of the book. A brief discussion of potential beneficiaries of a book on doing business in Kenya is offered. Chapter ends with discussion and conclusion sections. Kenya is an East African country with one of the fastest-growing economies in the region. We begin this section by providing a brief overview of Kenya within the African context.

1.2 Continent Context

Africa, the home of Kenya, is eliciting enthusiasm for business opportunities causing many business developers to think about the interesting investment prospects in this part of the world. Africa comprises 54 countries with a combined population of 1.3 billion people and some of the world's fastest-growing economies. Moreover, Africa is a vibrant continent with remarkable business opportunities (World Bank, 2021a). It is the second most populous continent in the world, after Asia. Indeed, in the last few years, Africa has recorded the highest population growth rate worldwide at 2.4 percent. The African continent is home to many young people. There are about 21 countries that have median populations of 18 and below. The continent's growing, youthful population amidst an aging population constitutes a formidable market. In addition, the youthful population also contributes to a plentiful labor force which ultimately ensures lower production costs. Furthermore, Africa presents strong evidence for massive entrepreneurship and innovation largely because of the unmet needs and unfulfilled demand.

It is projected that by the turn of the century, consumer spending in Africa will reach $2.5 trillion, with more than 20 percent of this spending occurring in Sub-Saharan Africa (Rand Merchant Bank, 2020). Mass urbanization occurring across the continent will further bolster consumer

DOI: 10.4324/9781003095156-1

spending. It is also worth noting that African countries have significantly improved their investment climate. In contrast, GDP growth and foreign direct investment flows have registered a consistent positive trajectory. According to the African Development Bank (2021), African economies are projected to grow 3.1 percent in 2021, rivaling many global economies.

Economic freedom, among other policy measures, has become a major attraction for doing business on this continent (World Bank, 2020a). The increase in GDP growth has resulted in increased disposable income, therefore, increasing the demand for many consumer products.

The large deposits of natural resources and predominant extractive sectors, including agriculture in the continent, are the key linchpins of the desired value chains (Rand Merchant Bank, 2020). It is also noteworthy that 60 percent of the world's uncultivated land is in Africa.

The African Continental Free Trade Area (AfCFTA) established under the auspices of the African Union, gives all member states, including Kenya, access to the continental market (African Union, 2021). AfCFTA seeks to improve the export capacity of both formal and informal service suppliers by reducing tariffs and simplifying trading regimes. Therefore, Kenyan entrepreneurs and businesses have access to the African potential continent market of 1.3 billion people and a combined gross domestic product (GDP) of UDS$ 3.4 trillion.

1.3 East Africa Regional Positioning

East Africa, the regional home for Kenya, has a population of 445,405,606 (International Monetary Fund, 2021a). Six countries of the region, that is, Burundi, Kenya, Rwanda, South Sudan, Tanzania and Uganda, with a population of about 195.3 million, have ratified a treaty to create the East African Community (EAC). This regional intergovernmental organization has established a customs union and free trade protocols for the member states. The EAC has been described as one of the fastest-growing blocs in a continent whose economic outlook is projected to rebound in 2021 due to vigorous domestic demand and public investments in infrastructure. Kenya is not only the strongest economy in the bloc, but it is also the second most populous country after Tanzania. It represents 46 percent of the region's GDP and 27.5 percent of the total population in the region (International Monetary Fund, 2021a).

1.4 The Country of Kenya Overview

1.4.1 Kenya – Physical Features

Kenya is bisected horizontally by the equator and vertically by longitude 38° E, bordering five countries (the Republic of Kenya, 2020). To the north, it borders South Sudan and Ethiopia; to the east is Somalia and

Figure 1.1 Map of Kenya.

the Indian Ocean, to the south is Tanzania and to the west is Lake Victoria and Uganda (Figure 1.1). Kenya has about 536 kilometers of coastline in the Indian Ocean. It covers an area of 225,000 square miles (582,646 square kilometers) It is approximately the size of the US State of Texas.

Kenya is endowed with a wide range of topographical features – from the low plains found along the coast, bisected by the Great Rift Valley, to the fertile plateau in the west. The Great Rift Valley is home to several lakes, arid and rugged landscapes, and volcanic landforms with areas of active hot springs and geothermal activity. The highland areas of Central Kenya provide fertile ground for farming, making Kenya one of the most agriculturally productive countries in Africa. However, northern Kenya is largely desert land with scattered thorn bushes. This contrasts greatly with the Kenyan coast, which features many beaches, coral reefs, creeks, and coral islands. The coastal strip is mostly flat, giving rise to the rolling Taita hills. Mount Kilimanjaro, Africa's highest mountain, is located along the border between Kenya and Tanzania. Mount Kenya, the second-highest mountain in Africa, is located in Kenya's former central and eastern provinces.

1.4.2 Kenya – Investment Environment

Viewed through the political, economic, social, technological, environmental and legal (PESTEL) framework, Kenya has made significant strides to improve the investment environment. *Doing Business 2020* posits that Kenya's business environment has improved progressively (World Bank, 2020a). Today, Kenya is economically open presenting a business infrastructure that promotes entrepreneurship and business development. Overall, Kenya's macroeconomic fundamentals are strong and are poised to improve over time. Furthermore, the government has implemented various business-oriented reforms which have strengthened the business infrastructure and boosted investors' confidence in Kenya (US Department of State, 2020).

Kenya has a vibrant telecommunications sector, a robust financial services industry, a developed logistics hub, a strong innovative culture and extensive aviation connections throughout Africa, Europe and Asia. Government investment in infrastructure, a relatively stronger economy compared to other African countries, an ideal location, ICT innovations, a vibrant private sector place Kenya in a strong competitive position compared to its neighbors. Kenya is also affiliated with several international organizations such as the World Bank Group, United Nations and the International Criminal Court. Nairobi, the capital city, is the headquarters of many international (e.g. UN Habitat), and regional organizations and businesses. For example, General Motors, Coca-Cola PLC, and Unilever have located their regional or pan-African operations in Kenya. Mombasa, its main port, is the gateway for most of the hinterland East and Central African trade. By virtue of Kenya being a member of the EAC, the Africa Continental Free Trade Area (AfCFTA), and other regional trade blocs provides growing access to larger regional markets. Over time, Kenya has become a center of innovation, especially in mobile phone-based financial services, leading to employment opportunities and reinvigorating economic growth.

1.4.3 Kenya – Economic Perspective

The economic landscape of Kenya is discussed extensively in Chapter 5 of this book. In this section, we present key highlights of the country's economy.

As noted earlier, Kenya is by far the largest economy in East Africa with a GDP of $105.7 billion (International Monetary Fund, 2021a) in 2020 representing 46 percent of the region's total GDP (Figure 1.2) almost equivalent to the next two largest economies combined. Next is Tanzania with 29 percent followed by Uganda at 18 percent. Rwanda, South Sudan and Burundi contributed 5 percent, 2 percent and 1 percent respectively to the region's GDP. Kenya's position as the economic, commercial and logistical hub in Eastern and Central Africa, places the country as one of the most competitive investment destinations globally. Equally important is the

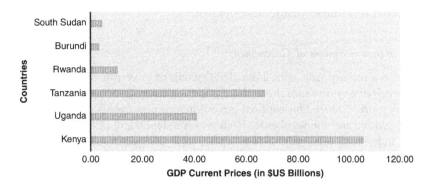

Figure 1.2 GDP Current Prices.

fact that Kenya is one of the world's 50 countries that have attained the lower middle-income status according to the World Bank GDP per capita threshold (World Bank, 2021b). Tanzania is the only other country in this region to achieve this status. The other 17 African countries in this GDP cluster include Angola, Algeria, Benin, Cameron, Cote d'Ivoire, Democratic Republic of Congo, Djibouti, Egypt, Ghana, Lesotho, Mauritius, Morocco, Nigeria, Senegal, Tunisia, Zambia and Zimbabwe. Kenya's expanded middle income population has stimulated economic development by enhancing domestic demand. With a decade of strong economic growth, Kenya has been rated as one of the fastest growing economies in Sub-Saharan Africa. GDP growth was projected at 5.5 percent in 2020 amid robust private consumption, higher credit growth and rising public and private investment; in addition, rapid urbanization and further regional integration that was expected to continue to open up investment opportunities (World Bank, 2021a). It is projected that Kenya's economy will rebound to approximately 7.6 percent in 2021, subject to the post-COVID-19 pandemic global economic recovery. Kenya is also uniquely distinguished from many African countries due to its diversified economy. More recently, the discovery of oil in Turkana in the northern part of the country is likely to strengthen and boost the country's economic growth. Key economic sectors include agriculture, forestry, fishing, mining, manufacturing, energy, tourism and financial services (Kenya National Bureau of Statistics, 2020).

In Sub-Saharan Africa, Kenya, which is often referred to as the "Silicon Savannah", is a leader in digitalization in both access to and use of digital technologies (Center for Global Development, 2019). Compared with other African countries, Kenya leads in the digital economy's contribution to GDP at 7.7 percent followed by Morocco and South Africa at 6.82 percent and 6.51 percent, respectively (World Bank, 2021a). For example, Kenya is the home of the first mobile money transfer innovation, M-pesa, and continues to occupy a leading position in digital technology in Africa.

This is driven by a wealth of technological expertise and government supported ICT infrastructure development.

1.4.4 Kenya – System of Government

Kenya is a unitary state with a devolved system of government comprising two levels of government: the national and the county governments (Kenya Law Report, 2020). The national government comprises of the judiciary, the executive and the legislature. Each arm is independent of the other and their individual roles. Significant service delivery functions vest in the counties.

Kenya's legal system is based on the English Common Law, and the 2010 constitution established an independent judiciary with a Supreme Court, Court of Appeal, Constitutional Court and High Court. For efficiency, the Employment and Labor Relations Court and the Milimani Commercial Courts have been created to expedite resolution of economic and commercial disputes. The business regulatory system is relatively transparent and continues to improve. Proposed laws and regulations pertaining to business and investment are published in draft form for public input and stakeholder deliberation before their passage into law. Furthermore, Kenya's environmental law has incorporated the principles of sustainable development by including public participation in environmental management.

1.4.5 Kenya – Size and Structure of Population

Kenya has a population of 53.8 million citizens (International Monetary Fund, 2021a) representing 12.2 percent of the Eastern African's population. According to the 2019 census, the population was 47.6 million with females accounting for 50.5 percent and males accounting for 49.5 percent (Kenya National Bureau of Statistics, 2020). Nairobi, the capital of Kenya, is the largest and most populous city, while Mombasa is the second largest and the country's main port. Based on the 2019 census, Kenya's population is predominantly youthful. Seventy five percent, approximately 35.7 million people, are below 35 years old. Thirty-nine percent of the total population is zero to 15 years. Thirty-six percent of the population is between 15 and 35 years, while 20 percent are over 35. With one of the highest literacy rates in the region at 88 percent, Kenya provides a large pool of highly qualified professionals in diverse sectors from a working population of over 47.5 percent out of a population of 53.8 million people (UNSECO Institute of Statistics, 2021).

1.4.6 Kenya Inflation and Unemployment Rate

The annual inflation of Kenya as measured by the consumer price index based on expenditures of both urban and rural households – increased from

5.3 percent in 2020 to 5.7 percent in 2021 (Central Bank of Kenya, 2021). In December 2020, the unemployment rate in Kenya rose to almost 2.86 percent up from 2.6 percent in 2019. In the long term, Kenya's unemployment rate is projected to trend around 12.3 percent in 2021 (International Monetary Fund 2021b).

1.5 Structure of the Book

This book consists of nine chapters, as discussed briefly in this section. This chapter will start with a brief introduction to the country Kenya. This is followed by a description of the book's structure, the country's background, and the importance of studying Kenya. This chapter will also highlight who will benefit from reading this book. This chapter also provides a substantive discussion of the state of business in Kenya.

Chapter 2 discusses the Kenyan business environment, Agenda 2030 Sustainable Development, and how it affects business. Furthermore, the authors outline the effects of the globalization phenomenon on market structures and business opportunities. This chapter also covers the regional as well as the Kenyan business environment. It also presents major business trends in Kenya by highlighting key successful industries. A substantive discussion of the impact of new business ideas, market restructuring, and business development is also presented.

Chapter 3 provides an overview of Kenya's economic landscape and its impact on business development. Kenya's legal system is examined as a basis of synthesizing the legal requirements for doing business in Kenya. The chapter also provides a succinct analysis of the plethora of laws that relate to business activity in Kenya with an emphasis on conflict resolution in business, property protection rights, contract enforcement and regimes of business formation. Types or forms of business ventures in Kenya, including proprietorships, partnerships, companies, cooperatives, and parastatals (state-owned corporations) are also discussed. The chapter concludes with financing options for business activities.

Most international investors analyze the PESTEL environment before entering a foreign market. Chapter 4 focuses primarily on the first part of the PESTEL analysis, namely the political environment. This chapter discusses the political system in Kenya and how it interfaces with business development and business activity. Political risk is examined for the reader to appreciate the political intricacies that impact business in Kenya. The chapter further explores the role of international treaties and illuminates obstacles to conducting business in Kenya. The chapter ends with a substantive discussion of the political situation in Kenya and its impact on the business environment.

Chapter 5 begins with a background of Kenya's economic systems. Economic policies, including monetary and fiscal strategies, are discussed in the context of business development. Issues such as import substitution and economic liberalization related to business development are discussed. An analysis of the country's stock exchange and financial market is presented. Finally, discussing how these issues affect present and future business activities is discussed.

Chapter 6 covers culture as a major factor in any business development. Foreign direct investment (FDI) relies on an accurate and proper understanding of how national cultures and subcultures affect business conduct in any country. The role of language, national culture, subcultures, religion, and interpersonal communication will be discussed in detail. Kenyan business customs and etiquette will also be examined. Explanations of how culture affects business development will be at the core of this chapter's discussion; as with previous chapters, a major discussion section will focus on why it is important to talk about culture and business development.

Chapter 7 provides a detailed approach to how to develop a business in Kenya. It delves into the steps necessary to initiate business development, and the resources, and institutions available during the business development process. Kenya's basic infrastructure and supply chain management will be discussed in this chapter, as well as the importance of corporate social responsibility and how it is actualized in Kenya. In addition, insurance options and implications are presented. The discussion section of this chapter will deliberate on the pros and cons of business development in Kenya.

Chapter 8 examines marketing in a Kenyan cultural context. Understanding how business marketing is done in Kenya is critical to appreciating how business is transacted in Kenya. A detailed analysis of the Kenyan marketing environment is developed. Marketing strategies that would be suitable and effective in Kenyan business ventures are discussed. This chapter analyzes the markets available to entrepreneurs and how marketing research can be conducted in Kenya. The adaptation of the marketing mix in Kenya is thoroughly discussed. Again, a substantive discussion of the marketing issues is part of this chapter.

Chapter 9 summarize why Kenya is a great choice for doing business. While the book has primarily examined current business practices, the book ends with an examination of new business opportunities in Kenya. The chapter examines the role of emerging technologies, disruptive business models such as the sharing economy, and other technological advances and how they collectively will change the face of business in Kenya. The role of these future business ventures and their impact on Kenya's economic development will be discussed as the book ends.

1.6 Why Study Kenya

There are many reasons to study Kenya's business environment. The first is to provide up-to-date information about the investment climate and an overview of doing business in Kenya to diverse audiences. This book contributes because it not only provides necessary information about the realities of doing business in Kenya but also contributes to existing literature. To our knowledge, existent books on doing business in Kenya are not readily available and are outdated.

Second, detailed information about the economic, social, technological, and cultural dimensions of society is discussed extensively. Together with the recommendations and suggestions offered, this book provides pertinent information regarding the paths an investor can pursue to establish a business venture in Kenya. Additionally, this book provides academics with a good understanding of the major issues affecting business development in Kenya.

Third, although Kenya might not be a perfect representation of Africa, it is an excellent location to learn about common business patterns and practices on the continent. In 2020, Kenya was ranked the third largest economy in Sub-Saharan Africa, after Nigeria and South Africa (The World Bank 2021, African Development Bank 2021). This knowledge helps potential investors and policymakers to make informed decisions. For researchers, the current work contributes to the study of African business models and theories. For Kenyan policymakers intent to make their country a more attractive destination to investors, this book provides invaluable information.

Fourth, considering the peaceful political atmosphere that prevails, the rich traditions and culture, the youthful and innovative human resources, the vast natural resources, and an investment climate ready for business, Kenya is uniquely positioned to compete in the international markets. Fifth, Kenya is a progressive country with a population with initiative, ambition and desire to improve their quality of life. It is a significant player in the region and the international arena. The continued prominence of Kenya in regional geopolitics has a great bearing on the country's overall development and investment attractiveness.

Sixth, Kenya's major country-specific characteristics include its free market philosophy, stable macroeconomic environment, economic performance, political stability, sizable domestic market, ease of access to regional markets of about 190 million people, communication efficiency, relatively better business infrastructure, dynamic, well-educated youthful population, a robust private sector as well as steady remittances inflows. Seventh, Kenya is one of the fastest-growing economies in Sub-Saharan Africa (The World Bank 2020), emerging as a dominant economic player not only in East Africa but also in the whole region. It is generally considered the economic, commercial, financial, and logistics hub of East Africa and is ranked as the most industrially developed country in the region. In addition, Kenya has a significant population (53.8 million in 2020), making it the second most populous country in East Africa after Tanzania and constituting 27.5 percent of the region's population.

1.7 Who Will Benefit

Very few people have a comprehensive understanding of the business development activities in Kenya. This book gives readers a wide-ranging view of business development and operations in Kenya. One of the biggest challenges in business and investment is the lack of adequate and accurate information. The authors know that consolidated information on Kenya's investment climate and business development in a single source is lacking. Investors, both domestic and foreign, who are looking for information to make investment decisions will find this book extremely useful. The book also discusses different business organizations and how they may be established. The authors present information on the current business landscape and analyze the investment climate. Foreign investors will find this analysis particularly informative as they consider their investment decisions.

Undergraduate and graduate students in business schools will find the book a valuable resource for their academic work. This book brings together business literature drawn from several sources while underscoring parallels from other countries, especially in Africa. While the focus is on Kenya, this book nonetheless helps the reader to understand common business models and practices across the continent of Africa.

Policymakers will see how current policies impact Kenya as a preferred investment destination.

1.8 Discussion

Kenya is a free-market capitalistic country with the largest economy in East Africa. It has made significant strides to improve its investment environment to gain a competitive edge as a formidable investment destination in Africa. In 2014, Kenya attained a lower middle-income status underscoring the economic development that the country has achieved.

Kenya is a democratic unitary state with a devolved system of government comprising two levels of government; the national and the county governments. The national government comprises three independent branches, that is, the executive, legislature, and judiciary. The executive arm enforces the law, the legislature makes laws, and the judiciary is responsible for applying and upholding the law. As one of the fastest-growing economies in Sub-Saharan Africa, Kenya enjoys a unique position to attract investment. This is underpinned by business-friendly policies, strong private consumption, higher credit growth, rising public and private investment, rapid urbanization, and superior communication infrastructure.

1.9 Conclusion

Kenya demonstrates a good case study as a surrogate of African business development. First, Africa presents lucrative business opportunities that are largely unexploited. Second, Kenya is not only the gateway and communications hub for Eastern and Central Africa, but it also has access potentially to the 1.3 billion people market. It has a promising economy with reforms supported by law that facilitate business operations and investments.

Its huge domestic consumption, reasonable disposable incomes, innovative and entrepreneurial culture, and abundant natural resources provide the impetus for business development.

References

African Development Bank. (2021). Africa's economic outlook 2021. https://www.afdb.org/sites/default/files/2021/03/09/aeo_2021_n.pdf

African Union. (2021). Africa's free trade area opens for business. Retrieved from https://www.un.org/africarenewal/magazine/january-2021/afcfta-africa-now-open-business

Center for Global Development. (2019). Digital technology and state capacity in Kenya. https://www.cgdev.org/sites/default/files/digital-technology-and-state-capacity-kenya.pdf

Central Bank of Kenya. (2021). Inflation rates. https://www.centralbank.go.ke/inflation-rates/

International Monetary Fund. (2021a). World economic outlook (October 2020). https://www.imf.org/external/datamapper/

International Monetary Fund. (2021b). Inflation: Prices on the rise. https://www.imf.org/external/pubs/ft/fandd/basics/pdf/oner_inflation.pdf

Kenya Law Report. (2020). Constitution of Kenya, 2010. Laws of Kenya. http://kenyalaw.org

Kenya National Bureau of Statistics. (2020). Economic survey 2020. https://www.knbs.or.ke/

Rand Merchant Bank. (2020). Where to invest in Africa 2020. https://www.rmb.co.za/landing/where-to-invest-in-africa

Republic of Kenya. (2020). General information about Kenya. The permanent mission of the republic of Kenya to the United Nations. https://www.un.int/kenya/kenya/general-information-about-kenyaUnitedNations. World Population Prospects https://esa.un.org/unpd/wpp/Publications/Files/WPP2020_DataBooklet.pdf

The World Bank. (2019). Kenya digital economy assessment report. http://pubdocs.worldbank.org/en/345341601590631958/DE4A-Kenya-summary-paper-final.pdf

The World Bank. (2020)Doing business 2020: Economy profile Kenya. https://openknowledge.worldbank.org/bitstream/handle/10986/32436/9781464814402.pdf

The World Bank. (2021a) The World Bank in Africa. https://www.worldbank.org/en/region/afr/overview

The World Bank. (2021b). Lower middle income. Retrieve from https://data.worldbank.org/country/XN

UNSECO Institute of Statistics. (2021). http://uis.unesco.org/en/glossary-term/literacy-rate#:~:text=Definition,to%20ages%2065%20and%20above

US Department of State. (2020). 2020 investment climate statements: Kenya. https://www.state.gov/reports/2020-investment-climate-statements/kenya/

2 Business Environment

2.1 Introduction

Kenya's business environment, as measured by the World Bank's *Ease of Doing Business* index, has shown progressive improvement for the last ten years, thus suggesting a bullish investment climate. In 2021, ease of doing business in Kenya was ranked 56th globally, and third best in Sub-Saharan Africa (World Bank, 2021a). Among Sub-Saharan African countries, Kenya's rank for starting a business was 25, while dealing with construction was 15, getting electricity was 3, registering property was 24, and getting credit was 3. The Heritage Foundation (2021) scores Kenya's business freedom at 55, labor freedom at 55.8, and monetary freedom at 75. Regardless of the progress, as mentioned earlier, Kenya will need to implement more reforms in different areas to attract more investments. A country's business environment is a critical factor that influences investment decisions. Research has shown a positive correlation between the level of investment and the business environment as measured by the Doing Business Index. The term 'business environment' refers to external factors and institutions that are beyond the control of the business and affect the functioning of the business (Richman & Copen, 1972). The business environment has also been defined as the 'climate' or set of conditions – economic, social, political or institutional – in which business operations are conducted (Weimer, 1970). Other external factors that comprise the business environment include customers, competitors, suppliers, government and technology.

2.2 Kenya's Business Environment

Kenya's business environment is generally viewed as friendly, providing several opportunities for investors. Like many other countries, however, Kenya's business typology is constantly changing despite these friendly conditions, which poses major threats that call for strategic management by business operators. The dynamic nature of the business environment is exacerbated by associated complexities that require businesses to continue to learn and adapt.

DOI: 10.4324/9781003095156-2

Kenya has a robust economy currently ranked as lower middle-income and boasts one of the strongest economies in the region (US Department of State, 2020). Additionally, Kenya has historically had a stable government modeled in a multi-party democracy with a relatively efficient legal system.

Other favorable factors are the country's strategic geographic location, sizable and diverse population, well-educated workforce, technological innovativeness, large market and strong international standing. Kenya has excelled in the tourism industry and draws a significant portion of its foreign exchange from tourism. The government has invested heavily in tourism, and the country continues to win international awards. For example, in 2020, Kenya was named Africa's leading tourist destination by the World Travel Awards. Kenya's spectacular flora and fauna and tropical climate are the country's main attractions. The Maasai Mara Game Reserve, Samburu National Reserve, Shimba Hills National Reserve, Sweet Waters Game Reserve, and Tsavo National Park are among Kenya's top safari destinations (Travel Noire 2020), while the Kenyatta International Convention Center was named Africa's leading meetings and conference center in 2020. Kenya also boasts some excellent hotels, with the Villa Rosa Kempinski in Nairobi being named Africa's leading luxury hotel and the Fairmount Mount Kenya Safari Club as Africa's leading standard hotel. The capital city of Nairobi was named Africa's leading business travel destination in 2020. Kenya Airways won Africa's leading airline in 2021. Also, in 2020, Kenya was named Africa's leading golfing destination at the UAE's annual World Golf Awards gala ceremony. Kenya was recognized for excellence in golf tourism and being a superior golf destination, beating out South Africa, Egypt and Morocco.

Kenya aims to rank among the top 30 most attractive investment destinations globally in the next decade (the Republic of Kenya, 2021a). Five key reasons investors should consider doing business in Kenya are as follows: (a) it is a market-based economy; (b) it is the economic, commercial, financial and logistics hub of East Africa; (c) it has a young and educated population that speaks English with high proficiency in technology; (d) it's continuous improvement in the ease of doing business and (e) its abundant endowment in natural resources. For a comprehensive analysis of the Kenyan business environment, we delineate the discussion into the following key areas: (i) physical location factors; (ii) economic factors; (iii) political and legal factors; (iv) infrastructure development; (v) facilitative and supportive institutions; (vi) socio-cultural factors; (vii) technology and innovation; and (viii) governance and security.

2.2.1 Physical Location Factors

In Chapter 1, we presented Kenya's diverse and spectacular physical features. On the one hand, the highlands and glaciers bestow an enormous amount of natural beauty to the country. On the other hand, the lowlands and seaside regions offer beautiful beaches and habitats for aquatic life. Kenya enjoys a tropical climate with a warm and humid coastal area. Rainfall in Kenya is seasonal, with long rains falling between April and June and short rains between October and December. Kenya's geographic location, physical features and climate present bountiful investment opportunities in agriculture, sporting and hospitality. Kenya also boasts a large consumer market (over 45 million inhabitants), as well as natural resources in the form of arable land, wildlife and minerals (Kenya Investment Authority 2021a). In addition, Kenya is generally considered the economic, commercial, financial and logistics hub of East Africa (US Department of State, 2020) because of its strategic location, relatively superior infrastructure, and human capital. Moreover, Kenya's Port of Mombasa serves as a gateway entry and exit point for Kenya, Uganda, Burundi, Tanzania, the Democratic Republic of the Congo, Somalia, and Ethiopia (Kenya Ports Authority).

2.2.2 Economic Factors

2.2.2.1 Competitiveness and Ease of Doing Business

A country's competitiveness includes the following: (a) its ability to provide an enabling environment for firms to improve and innovate faster than foreign rivals; (b) its economic conditions and their influence on competitiveness; (c) the efficiency of the legal environment; (d) maintenance of a high level of social welfare of citizens; and (e) a set of institutions, policies and factors that determine the level of productivity of a country (Petryle, 2017). In 2020, Kenya scored 54.1 on the Global Competitiveness Index and ranked 56th globally, becoming the third most competitive country in Sub-Saharan Africa (World Bank, 2020).

Kenya's economic freedom score was 55.3 out of 100, compared to the world average of 61.6, while trade freedom was 60.4, investment freedom 55, and financial freedom 50. These numbers can be explained by persistent inefficiencies and a lack of transparency, which may discourage investment activity (Heritage Foundation, 2021). The government, however, is focused on making Kenya a secure and attractive investment destination through continuous improvement of the business environment. To this end, several policies have promoted business activity, including the country's development blueprint, Vision 2030. Currently, the government is implementing the third of its 5-year medium plans, 'The Third Term Medium Term Plan' (MTP III), which aims to enhance Kenya's economic growth and other sector-specific reforms like tax incentives and an improved business environment.

2.2.2.2 Economic Conditions

Kenya's economy is market-based with liberalized international trade, and is discussed comprehensively in Chapter 5. Following the COVID-19 pandemic recovery, Kenya's economy is projected to rebound to approximately seven percent (World Bank, 2021a). Macroeconomic stability provides the environment necessary for private sector investments that fuel sustained economic growth. From a policy standpoint, Kenya will need to maintain macroeconomic stability by pursuing prudent fiscal and monetary policies that will stimulate the economy and grow businesses.

As articulated in Vision 2030, Kenya's future economic growth is based on robust private consumption, higher credit growth, and rising public and private investment. In addition, rapid urbanization and further regional integration are expected to open up investment opportunities (Kenya Vision 2030). This was reinforced by President Uhuru Kenyatta's 'Big 4' agenda, which focused on enhancing food security, manufacturing, universal health coverage and affordable housing. In August 2022, President William Samoei Ruto became the 5th President of Kenya and his Kenya Kwanza party has adopted a "bottom up economic model "comprised of six pillars. These six pillars are: Agriculture; Micro, Small and Medium Enterprise (MSME) economy; Housing and Settlement; Healthcare; Digital superhighway and creative economy; Environment and climate change. The bottom up model will ultimately bring down the cost of living, eradicate hunger, create jobs, expand the tax base and improve the country's foreign exchange balance. In recent years, Kenya's business environment has been significantly enhanced (Khawaja et al., 2020), partly because the government recognizes the critical role of private sector investors in this economic development. Kenya enjoys a steadily growing economy stronger than other countries in the surrounding regions. In 2020, Kenya was ranked the third largest economy in Sub-Saharan Africa, after Nigeria and South Africa (Mboya, 2020). Since 2014, Kenya has been ranked as a lower-middle-income country based on its GDP per capita (World Bank, 2021a). Key economic sectors that Kenya will need to leverage include agriculture, forestry, fishing, mining, manufacturing, energy, tourism and financial services.

2.2.2.3 Inflation and Interest Rates

Kenya's inflation rate of 5.3 percent in 2021 was relatively better than the Sub-Saharan African average of 7.3 percent (Central Bank of Kenya, 2021a). The major driver of overall inflation has been food inflation. Kenya's overarching policy objective is to maintain low and stable interest rates to support access to credit. In 2021, the Central Bank rate was fixed at 7 percent, while the interbank rate was set at 5.2 percent to ease monetary policy and provide adequate liquidity. Going forward, the government must consistently employ appropriate monetary and fiscal policies to maintain interest rates at reasonably low levels.

2.2.2.4 Unemployment and Population

In 2020, Kenya's unemployment rate was about 10.4 percent and was projected to rise to 12.3 percent in 2021 (International Monetary Fund,

2021), which is of major concern. Kenya has a population of 53.8 million (World Bank, 2020), representing 12.2 percent of Eastern Africa's population, providing a potentially huge domestic market and ample labor force. Kenya also has access to the African market by the African Continental Free Trade Area (AfCFTA) and the East African Community (EAC) free trade protocols, thus reaching an additional 1.3 billion people (International Monetary Fund, 2020).

2.2.2.5 Investment Incentives

The government of Kenya has implemented sector-specific investment incentives, including an investment deduction of 100 percent for the hospitality and manufacturing industries, 10 percent for local film producers and a 150 percent investment allowance for manufacturing operations situated outside of Kisumu, Mombasa, and Nairobi (Kenya Revenue Authority, 2020). Enterprises operating in export processing zones (EPZs) enjoy a ten-year tax holiday. The EPZ promotes and facilitates export-oriented investments and has developed an enabling environment for such investments. These enterprises are exempt from several taxes and duties including (a) excise duties; (b) income tax for the first ten years from the date of the first sale as an EPZ enterprise; (c) withholding tax on dividends and other payments made to non-residents; and (d) stamp duty (Export Processing Zones Authority, 2021). Enterprises in special economic zones (SEZs) are subject to a reduced corporate tax rate between 10 percent and 15 percent. Like the EPZ firms, SEZ enterprises are also eligible for a 100 percent investment deduction on buildings, plants and machinery used in manufacturing. Current SEZs include the Naivasha Industrial Park, the Dongo Kundu Special Economic Zone in the coastal region and the Kisumu Special Economic Zone in Miwani (Republic of Kenya, 2021b).

2.2.2.6 Financial Services

In this section, the key aspects of Kenya's financial services sector will be covered and are discussed substantively in Chapter 5. This sector comprises the banking, insurance, capital markets, pension, and Sacco societies subsectors. All of these entities adhere to international standards while utilizing modern technology, meaning that the financial services sector in Kenya is generally stable.

Eighty-three percent of Kenyan adults have a formal account for saving, sending, and receiving money (Central Bank of Kenya, 2021b). There are 42 commercial banks with several micro-finance and digital credit institutions, as well as investment banks with a robust capital market operating in Kenya, making it the leader in financial services in the region. Furthermore, Kenya is the leading country in access to credit globally (World Bank, 2020). The banking sector is stable and resilient and is recognized as a major promoter of

Kenya's economic development. Several reforms have been instituted to bolster financial services in Kenya, such as the Nairobi International Financial Center, which was established to strengthen the business environment by making conducting financial services and related activities in Kenya it more efficient, thereby increasing capital inflow for investments and creating new financing options (Republic of Kenya, 2021c). Other reforms include a government-supported credit guarantee scheme for small and medium-sized enterprises, ramping up compliance with international standards on anti-money laundering and combating the financing of terrorism, and establishing a digital finance grid. Through these reforms, various financing activities that were previously restricted now provide the flexibility and incentives to invest in business ventures (Khawaja et al., 2020).

2.2.2.7 Public Expenditure

Public expenditure as a driver for economic growth is also discussed in Chapter 5. In this section, Kenya's public expenditure and its implications for business development are discussed. Government spending was 26.1 percent of GDP over the previous three years, and budget deficits have averaged 7.8 percent of GDP (Central Bank of Kenya, 2021c). Public debt was equivalent to 65.7 percent of GDP at the end of June 2020 because of high deficits and large public infrastructure spending, exacerbating the already fragile public debt distress risk. The tax burden was estimated at 78.7 percent, government spending at 78.6 percent, and fiscal health at 13.5 percent (Kenya National Bureau of Statistics, 2021). The high public expenditure and huge public debt levels not only stifle economic growth but also subdue private sector credit growth and curtail investment activities. The sustainability of Kenya's current public debt is debatable. Still, the Kenyan government is expected to maintain a sustainable debt level long-term through its public debt and borrowing policies (the Republic of Kenya, 2021c).

2.2.3 Political/Legal Factors

2.2.3.1 Structure of Government and International Relations

In this section, a summary of Kenya's political and legal structure is provided; however, a comprehensive analysis of Kenya's government structure is to be found in Chapters 1 and 4. Kenya is a multiparty democracy whose system of government comprises three branches – the executive, the legislature, and the judiciary. After passing the 2010 Constitution, Kenya currently has two levels of government consisting of national and county governments (Kenya Law, 2021a). Consistent political stability and peace throughout the years also provide confidence for investors.

Kenya is a member of over 60 international organizations, including the United Nations; the UN Security Council; the International Monetary Fund;

the African Development Bank; the African Union; EAC; Common Market for Eastern and Southern Africa (COMESA); World Bank; World Trade Organization; African Union; and the Organization of African, Caribbean and the Pacific States. These affiliations elevate Kenya's international standing and bolster investors' confidence in the country (Kenya Law, 2021b).

2.2.3.2 Business Laws

Kenya's legal framework is discussed extensively in Chapter 3. Therefore, this section will only cover some aspects of Kenya's business law, including business registration, contracts, intellectual property rights, and employment law.

Business Registration: A well-functioning regulatory framework minimizes the costs of business formation, operation, and closure. Rules governing business entry and the different types of business organizations are vital for encouraging entrepreneurship, investment, and business operations. To improve the investment climate, Kenya has implemented several reforms, including re-engineering business registration, licensing, payment of taxes, and monitoring (the Republic of Kenya, 2021a). Some automation of registration processes has also ramped up the legal and policy framework for business registration. In addition, relevant laws and processes have been streamlined, reducing numerous cumbersome procedures and the number of business licenses (the Republic of Kenya, 2021a). For example, four separate registration steps with the Registry of Business, Kenya Revenue Authority, National Hospital Insurance Fund, and National Social Security Fund were previously required; now, they have been consolidated, and two others were eliminated. Furthermore, the Business Registration Service provides a mechanism for businesses to enter one-day, one-step registration process. These improvements have significantly helped increase entrepreneurial incentives and business development activity (Khawaja et al., 2020).

Contract Enforcement and Property Rights: Contract enforcement is recognized as an important aspect of doing business. Efficient resolution of business disputes encourages new investments and promotes speedy trials, saving businesses money in litigation. To this end, Kenya has introduced a case management system for commercial dispute resolution to enforce contracts more efficiently. Kenya ranked number 89 in 2020, up from position 149 in 2012, in enforcing contracts (World Bank, 2020). Kenya has a robust intellectual property legislative framework, as well as dedicated agencies that protect intellectual property. Despite these measures, cases of counterfeit goods are fairly common. The counterfeit market is expected to diminish with efforts to scale capacity in relevant institutions. The integrity of land registration and ownership is improving through the National Land Information Management System, with titles being digitized and registration automated (the Republic of Kenya, 2021c). This endeavor is geared toward enhancing the security of land records, improving accessibility and reducing the cost of land transactions; however, more land reforms may be needed to make Kenya more competitive.

Employment Law. This section consists of a general overview of Kenya's employment legal framework since human resources are a critical component of business activity. In Kenya, employment is a contractual relationship negotiated between the employee and the employer. This employment contract is governed by the general law of contract, as well as the principles of common law. Several laws specifically deal with different aspects of the employer-employee relationship, including defining the terms and conditions of employment. Wages (including minimum wages), housing, leave, health and safety, and termination are governed by the Employment Act and the Wages and Conditions of Employment Act. The Factories Act deals with the health, safety, and welfare of employees who works in a factory. The modalities of compensating an employee who is injured while on duty are governed by the Workmen's Compensation Act. There are 11 public paid holidays, including New Year's Day, Good Friday, Easter Monday, Labour Day, Eid-ul-Fitr-Day, Madaraka Day, Huduma Day, Mashujaa Day, Jamhuri Day, Christmas Day and Utamaduni Day (Kenya Law, 2021a). When any of these holidays falls on a Sunday, the next working day will be a holiday. The Constitution guarantees several freedoms and rights for individuals under the Bill of Rights, which makes it possible for employees to organize trade unions. Kenya's trade unions are fairly robust and are embedded in various statutes, including the Trade Unions Act, the Trade Disputes Act, and the Industrial Relations Charter. The resolution of disputes relating to employment and labor relations rests in the Industrial Court, which is a superior court of record. Key institutions relating to employment and labor in Kenya are the responsible government department, the Central Organization of Trade Unions, and the Federation of Kenyan Employers.

2.2.4 Infrastructure Development

Adequate and efficient infrastructure is critical for attracting investments because it stimulates economic growth. For this reason, the government should emphasize improving road networks, electricity distribution, rail networks, and water resources, among others. Good roads and railways ensure that goods will be easily transported to destination markets at competitive transport costs. Reduced transportation costs mean lower production costs and better prices for consumers, which will translate to higher consumption and a further increase in national output.

With about 177,800 roads, of which only 63,575 kilometers are classified, Kenya possesses a superior road network compared to its neighbors (the Republic of Kenya, 2021c). Its transportation infrastructure remains inadequate, however, and is a key obstacle to economic development. According to the USA Department of Commerce (2020), for Kenya to retain its current position, the government must enhance investment in its transportation infrastructure over the next decade. Several roads are under construction, including the Nairobi Expressway and the Nairobi-Mau Summit ExpressWay, Africa's largest private-public partnership project. The Dongo Kundu Southern Bypass, the Horn of Africa Gateway Development Project, Mau Mau Road, and the Kenol Sagana-Marua Road (Republic of Kenya, 2021c).

Kenya's rail network has a total of 2,778 kilometers of narrow gauge railway that links the Port of Mombasa and Malaba at the Kenya/Uganda border and a 579-kilometer standard gauge railway line between Mombasa and Nairobi. The SGR – Mombasa to Nairobi is the most expensive infrastructure project the Kenyan government has undertaken since its independence. The second phase of a 120 kilometers standard-gauge railway line from Nairobi to Naivasha is underway. Additional networks in the Lamu Port, South Sudan, and Ethiopia Transport Corridor are in the pipeline. Other meter gauge railways networks are undergoing rehabilitation, including the Nairobi-Nanyuki line and the Naivasha Kisumu line. This will not only improve the transportation of goods and passengers in Kenya but also in the neighboring countries of Uganda, Rwanda, Burundi, and the Democratic Republic of Congo.

Kenya's sole seaport in Mombasa is the largest port in East Africa and the second largest in Africa, serving Kenya and its neighboring countries (Uganda, Rwanda, South Sudan, Tanzania, Burundi, and the Democratic Republic of Congo). The Kenya Ports Authority is the government agency dedicated to maintaining, operating, improving, and regulating scheduled seaports along Kenya's coastline. Recent developments to improve the ports' capacity include the modernization of the Kilindini Harbor, the Lamu Port Berth-One, and the installation of the Likoni Floating Bridge. The Port of Kisumu is also under rehabilitation to harness the inter-country transport and trade potential within the East African region (Republic of Kenya, 2021c).

Kenya has international airports in Nairobi, Mombasa, Eldoret, and Kisumu. There are also domestic airports in Nairobi, Malindi, Lamu, and Lokichogio, and another 463 aerodromes and airstrips. The Kenya Airports Authority manages all public airport facilities (KAA). The KAA is the government agency in charge of with administering, controlling and managing aerodromes in the country (Kenya Airports Authority, 2021). Several airports are undergoing modernization and rehabilitation. The Jomo Kenyatta International Airport (JKIA) in Nairobi is the continent's premier hub and ideal gateway into and out East and Central Africa. JKIA is Kenya's largest aviation facility and the busiest airport in the region.

Abundant electrical energy is one of the most important drivers of any economic activity. Kenya's 2,150 megawatts of generation capacity, serving a population of more than 45 million, is inadequate, thus constraining economic growth. Kenya is believed to possess significant reservoirs of undeveloped geothermal energy resources in the Rift Valley, as well as wind and biomass energy. The government is focused on sustaining a stable investment climate by encouraging private-sector participation in the energy sector. The government is also developing expanded transmission and distribution networks to deliver needed power to customers. Furthermore, there is a strong commitment to maintaining cost-reflective tariffs and reducing inefficiencies in the sector to support more affordable end-user tariffs (the Republic of Kenya, 2021c).

2.2.5 Facilitative Institutions

In this section, some key institutions that support and facilitate investments and business operations in Kenya are discussed, as these institutions play facilitative and promotional roles.

a   *Ministry of Industrialization, Trade, and Enterprise Development*: This is the government department responsible for trade policy, development of retail and wholesale markets, business registration services and export promotion. It also deals with fair trade practices, coordination of regional trade matters, trade negotiations and advisory services, and enforcement of international trade laws, regulations and agreements. Other functions for this ministry include industrialization and cooperative policy formulation and implementation; implementation of the industrial property rights regime; private sector development policy and strategy; and quality control, including industrial standards development (the Republic of Kenya, 2021d).

b   *EPZ Authority*: This is the government agency responsible for promoting and facilitating export-oriented investments, as well as developing an enabling environment for such investments (Export Processing Zones Authority, 2021).

c   *Kenya Accreditation Service (KENAS)*: This is a government agency that gives formal attestation that Conformity Assessment Bodies are competent to carry out specific conformity assessment activities. KENAS is a member of the International Accreditation Forum and an associate member of the International Laboratory Accreditation Cooperation, both of which are apex organizations that oversee accreditation activities globally (the Republic of Kenya, 2021d).

d   *Kenya Investment Authority*: This is a government agency whose responsibility is to promote investments in Kenya by facilitating the implementation of new investment projects, providing aftercare services for new and existing investments, and organizing investment promotion activities both locally and internationally (Kenya Investment Authority, 2021b).

e   *Kenya National Chamber of Commerce and Industry*: This is a private-sector membership-based trade support institutions were working to protect the commercial and industrial interests of the Kenyan business community (Kenya National Chamber of Commerce and Industry, 2021).

f   *Kenya Bureau of Standards*: This is a government agency whose mandate is to provide the country with quality infrastructure for the facilitation of trade, support of industries and sustainability of production systems (Kenya Bureau of Standards, 2021).

g   *Kenya Association of Manufacturers*: This association represents manufacturing and value-added industries in Kenya. KAM drives policy advocacy toward the formation of industrial policies to strengthen and support the country's economic development (Kenya Association of Manufacturers, 2021).

h   *Kenya Private Sector Alliance*: This is the private sector apex and umbrella body that brings together the business community to engage and influence public policy for an enabling business environment (Kenya Private Sector Alliance, 2021).

i   *Private Public Partnership Directorate*: This is a government agency under the National Treasury. The PPP Directorate facilitates the implementation of the PPP program projects in Kenya by providing support to implementing agencies throughout the various stages of an infrastructure project's life cycle (the Republic of Kenya, 2021e).

j   *SEZ Authority*: This government institution is responsible for attracting, facilitating, and retaining domestic and foreign direct investments (FDIs) in SEZs. The agency exists to create an enabling environment for investors through the development of integrated infrastructure facilities, as well as the creation of incentives that eliminate the barriers to doing business (the Republic of Kenya, 2021d).

2.2.6 Socio-Cultural Dimension and Population

Kenya's socio-cultural dimension is discussed extensively in Chapter 6. This section summarizes this dimension. Kenya is a country with a diverse population of several different racial and ethnic groups. While English and Kiswahili are the official languages, over forty-two different tribal languages are spoken in Kenya. The diversity of the population has led to various opinions and actions related to Kenya's business development. It has given Kenya prominence on the African continent as one of the most promising countries for business and economic development.

Many investors want to work in environments where the labor force is well-educated and trained. The overall literacy rate for Kenya is 81.5 percent, with 85 percent literacy for men and only 78.2 percent for women (The World Factbook, 2021). However, these rates will continue to improve since the government is committed to providing free education for all. For example, in Kenya's Vision 2030, the government has identified human resource development as a key to transforming its economy toward that of a middle-income country (Kenya Vision, 2030, 2020). Additionally, the net student enrollment rate in primary schools was 99.6 percent in 2020, while a transition from primary to secondary schools was 100 percent in 2021 (the Republic of Kenya, 2021f). Increased labor productivity means increased production in an economy, further stimulating economic growth.

2.2.7 Technology and Innovation

Information Communication and Technology (ICT) is an indispensable tool in the highly globalized knowledge economy. ICT can improve market access by facilitating communication with customers, competitive positioning, and enabling information acquisition, and production of quality products. ICT can also enable companies to generate quality market data, reduce logistics costs, facilitate access to global markets, simplify market research, enhance networking, improve market transactions and help with market identification.

In Sub-Saharan Africa, Kenya is often referred to as the 'Silicon Savannah.' Kenya is a leader in digitalization, both in terms of access to and use of digital technologies (Center for Global Development, 2019). Compared with other African countries, Kenya is the leader in the digital economy's contribution to GDP, coming in at 7.7 percent, followed by Morocco and South Africa at 6.82 percent and 6.51 percent, respectively (World Bank, 2021a). Furthermore, Kenya is the home of the first mobile money transfer innovation, M-Pesa, and continues to occupy a leading position in digital technology in Africa. This is driven by a wealth of technological expertise and massive government investment in undersea fiber optic cables that boost Internet connectivity and reliability. This is expected to grow even more with the construction of the proposed Konza Technopolis Complex and the Konza Data Centre, as well as the Smart City Facilities Project (the Republic of Kenya, 2021c).

2.2.8 Governance and Security

Governance consists of many interdependent factors that together make up a framework allowing enterprises, investors, and entrepreneurs to engage in activities that enhance competitiveness. Some dimensions of governance include the following: (a) formal rule-bound governance; (b) the credibility of policies implemented by political authorities; and (c) the quality and honesty of bureaucratic agencies (OECD Development Centre, 2003). Weak legal systems breed opportunistic behavior if unethical conduct is not punished. This often snowballs into heightened informality, increased gatekeeping, and restricted business activities. Related to unethical behavior, corruption and bribery are illegal in Kenya, but together with weak governance, they undermine economic development. High levels of corruption in Kenya's public services are often reported in the media and have been an elusive menace to control. Kenya's corruption perceptions index was 28 in 2019, up from 27 the previous year. At the same time, Kenya was ranked the 138th least corrupt of 180 countries evaluated (Transparency International, 2021).

The Kenyan government has employed various measures to combat corruption, including enhancing capacity in the Office of the Director of Public Prosecutions, the Office of the Auditor General, the Ethics and Anti-Corruption Commission, the Assets Recovery Agency, the Criminal Investigations Services and the Financial Reporting Centre, in addition to the courts of law (the Republic of Kenya, 2021c). To improve the administration of justice, physical infrastructure for the courts has been expanded to include the creation of mobile courts, automation of court processes, digitization of judicial systems, adoption of virtual courts, the entrenchment of alternative dispute resolution initiatives (e.g., mediation and arbitration), clearance of case backlogs and improvement in case management in courts. In addition, some reforms have been undertaken by the government toward improving the public procurement system.

While insecurity deters business and investment development, good security creates a conducive business environment that attracts foreign investment. In Kenya, security is managed by national security institutions which, among others, address threats to security that undermine peace and development, including terrorism, radicalization and crime (Republic of Kenya, 2021c). Reported episodes of insecurity and crime in Kenya are prevalent in urban areas. Terrorism is a global security concern, and associated acts of terrorism often result in the destruction of property, loss of lives, reduced foreign investment, and diversion of public funds from otherwise high priority areas. In Kenya, most of these attacks are usually instigated by the Al-Shabaab militias, who operate predominantly from neighboring Somalia. Kenya will need to implement strong counter-terrorism strategies in a sustained manner to curtail terrorism.

2.3 Globalization of Business Environment

Globalization may be defined as a process of integration and inter-dependence among people, corporations, and countries to facilitate international trade and the flow of investment, labor and technology (Peterson Institute for International Economics, 2018). It has also been described as the process encompassing the political, economic and cultural integration of nations and peoples into a global community, thereby promoting convergence, harmonization, efficiency, growth, and perhaps, democratization and homogenization. Historically, globalization has brought together countries via more liberal cross-border trading activities. Globalization enhances the connectivity and interdependence of world markets and businesses, thus increasing competition. During the last two decades, globalization has accelerated advanced technology development and use, which in turn has made it easier for people to travel anywhere in the world.

Moreover, globalization has progressed rapidly due to significant improvements in advanced telecommunications infrastructure and, of course the Internet. Suffice it to say, the major forces driving economic globalization are as follows: information technology; economic liberalization; ease of global movement of capital; FDI and labor; integration of nations into free trade blocs; institutions such as the International Monetary Fund, World Trade Organization and World Bank; and expansion of transnational corporations (Naz and Ahmad, 2018).

2.4 Globalization and Its Implications

The debate on the implications of globalization has been ongoing and controversial. While Liu Zhenmin, UN Under Secretary (2021), acknowledges that globalization has promoted increased economic growth, expanding the global GDP by about 20 percent between 2000 and 2016, he also considers the associated shortcomings and disadvantages experienced by some countries. Similarly, Ngozi and Coulibaly (2019) contend that globalization supports knowledge transfer, helping Africa to improve its standards of living, but at the same time, causes such problems as premature deindustrialization, erosion of sovereignty, climate change, inequality and poverty, and denial to some host countries – usually African nations – their due share of the benefits of globalization.

Furthermore, most African economies, including Kenya, have not fully exploited the opportunities provided by globalization (Manda and Sen, 2004). This may be explained by several reasons, including the following: high reliance on primary commodity exports, insufficient export diversification; weak governance; poor physical infrastructure; and an unfavorable investment climate. Other reasons suggested are neo-colonial and imperialist practices, inadequate participation in international economic decision-making, poor technology, vulnerability to external shocks as a result of an unstable international economic and financial system, adverse economic and trade policies, falling terms of trade and asymmetrical trade relations between rich and poor nations (UNCTAD, 2016).

The future of globalization also remains in debate. Altman and Bastian (2021) note that cross-border flows dwindled in 2020 as the COVID-19 pandemic ravaged the world, casting doubts on the prospects of globalization. They conjecture that post-pandemic global business will rebound, though the landscape is expected to shift, with significant implications for management and strategic planning. Diversification in production locations, both domestic and foreign, driven by efficiency together with investments in technology and inventory, is also projected to increase.

The actions and relationships between major economies impact globalization significantly. Take the United States and China as an examples: despite the lingering United States-China trade wars, these two economies remain highly interdependent. China's share of US trade grew during the pandemic, and American multinational corporations such as Disney, Tesla, Starbucks, and Walmart continue to increase their presence in China (Altman and Bastian, 2021).

Furthermore, regional trade agreements concluded in the past year strongly suggest that globalization is poised to grow even stronger. The Regional Comprehensive Economic Partnership was signed in 2020 and covered the Asia–Pacific region, which controls almost one-third of the global economy. Other trade agreements the AfCFTA will further strengthen globalization.

Kenya has been progressively integrating into the global economy through economic liberalization policies entailing privatization of state corporations, price decontrols, floating the foreign exchange rate, eliminating trade barriers and opening up to competition, among others (Manda and Sen, 2004). Since 1988, the Kenyan government has implemented a series of measures to enhance investments, particularly tax incentives, reduction of trade licenses, efficiency enhancements for starting businesses, and export-oriented promotions (EPZs and SEZs). Kenya is also pursuing economic cooperation geared toward scaling up its global economic position through treaties and trade agreements for international trade. These include the East African Community Free Trade area, AfCFTA, and Africa Growth Act (AGOA).

Responses to the impact globalization have had on Kenya like in many other countries, are mixed. There is no question that Kenya has achieved economic growth during the last two decades, owing partially to globalization. Furthermore, there is no denying that overall, globalization has made a positive impact on Kenya's GDP, including propelling Kenya to become a middle-income economy (World Bank, 2021a). Anecdotal evidence suggests Kenya's economy has benefited from globalization; however, Manda and Sen (2004) found contrary to the notion that globalization contributes to economic growth, manufacturing employment deteriorated. In addition, globalization contributes to adverse labor market outcomes in Kenya. Therefore, globalization will need to be decoupled to determine its full effect on Kenya's economic development.

Globalization activities associated with exports and imports in Kenya have been severely impacted by the COVID-19 pandemic, causing a ripple effect throughout the economy (Bellamy, 2020). Policymakers have thus had to reshape their decisions and think about short-term and long-term impacts. Furthermore, Kenya, and indeed the entire continent of Africa, need to strategize about how to react to the reconfiguring of global value chains to continue benefitting from globalization. Re-energizing the globalization process without exposing citizens to negative effects on their health and well-being is critical.

2.5 Regional Business Environment

Although integration in Africa is relatively lower than in developed economies, there are strong indications for more and stronger regional integration across the continent. In the past two decades, Kenya has aggressively pursued regional integration through various regional trading blocs and arrangements, including the EAC; the COMESA; the Inter-Governmental Authority on Development (IGAD); the Community of Sahel–Saharan States (Cen-Sad); the AfCFTA; and the Tripartite Free Trade Area, the proposed free trade agreement between COMESA, SDAC and EAC (Republic of Kenya, 2021g). Kenya is also a member of bilateral trade protocols with several countries, including the European Union and the United States.

The EAC, comprising Burundi, Kenya, Rwanda, South Sudan, Tanzania and Uganda, with a total population of approximately 177 million, is a major market for Kenya's products, creating many opportunities for cross-border investment and trade (Republic of Kenya, 2021h). Furthermore, the EAC is leading in Africa in regional integration and free movement of goods and people (Africa Regional Integration Index, 2021). The COMESA bloc has a population of approximately 540 million, while the whole continent of Africa has a population of over 1.3 billion, providing a huge potential market for Kenya.

In Africa, regional integration is measured by the African Union Commission, United Nations Economic Commission for Africa, and the African Development Bank through the Africa Regional Integration Index along the following five dimensions: trade integration, productive integration, macroeconomic integration, infrastructural integration and free movement of people (Africa Regional Integration Index, 2021). Overall, South Africa is the best integrated country in Africa, followed by Kenya, with an integration index of 0.63 and 0.44, respectively. In 2019, integration in the EAC was ranked stronger than the Southern African Development Community (SADC), i.e., 0.54 against 0.53. Africa's largest bloc, the Cen-Sad, whose membership is from 27 countries in the northern part of the continent, including Kenya, was ranked worst with an index of 0.39. One of the key reasons for this poor performance is the communication barrier – the bloc uses up to four different official languages, i.e., Arabic, Portuguese, English, and French.

Kenya was ranked the leading performer in both the COMESA and EAC blocs, second best in IGAD, and 16 in Cen-Sad (Africa Regional Integration Index, 2021). While Kenya ranked well above the continental average in trade integration, productive integration, free movement of people, and infrastructural integration, its performance in macroeconomic integration was poor. This suggests that Kenya acknowledges the importance of regional integration as a means of more cross-border trade and investment.

Some key trade statistics demonstrate the economic significance of regional integration to Kenya. Africa contributed 38.2 percent to Kenya's total export earnings in 2020, making Africa Kenya's largest market (Kenya National Bureau of Statistics, 2021). The value of Kenya's exports to Africa increased by 9.8 percent to $USD 2.5 billion in 2020 from $USD 2.2 billion in 2019. With AfCTA coming into force in January 2021, Kenya's volume of business with the African continent can only improve.

Export earnings from the EAC into Kenya went up by 12.7 percent to $USD 1.6 billion in 2020 from $USD 1.4 billion in 2019, accounting for 64.3 percent of the total exports to Africa (Kenya National Bureau of Statistics, 2021). The markets that largely contributed to this increase are Rwanda, Uganda and South Sudan, whose exports increased by 20.8 percent. Uganda remained Kenya's largest export destination, representing 29.3 percent of Kenya's total exports to Africa. Furthermore, the value of Kenya's exports to COMESA rose from $USD 1.6 billion in 2019 to $USD 1.9 billion in 2020. Additionally, the value of exports to Nigeria increased by 43.3 percent to $USD 40 million in 2020 from $USD 28 million in 2019. Imports from Africa into Kenya dropped by 20.9 percent to $USD 1.8 billion in 2020.

Benefits accruing from regional integration include a wider market, the capacity to safeguard the region from international economic shocks, a common external tariff to protect domestic industries, cross-border travel efficiency, preferential tariff rates for exports and imports among member countries, and enhancement of regional infrastructural development (Republic of Kenya, 2021h). To reap these benefits, however, African countries need to allow the free movement of people, which will, in turn, enable traders and investors to operate beyond their national borders. Finally, Africa must trade with itself more than at the current rate. Information technology will also need to be enhanced to facilitate trade and investment and promote the continent's economic development and welfare.

2.6 Major Trends in Business Activity in Kenya

2.6.1 Government Initiatives

Kenya is the focal point for economic and business activity in the Eastern African region. By virtue of Kenya's superior stature, it is also experiencing a strong flow of FDI, with the majority of foreign investment expanding in the finance, insurance, renewable energy, trade, manufacturing, communication, and education industries (International Trade Administration, 2021). This may be explained by the fact that Kenya has ambitiously focused on improving the ease of doing business through a broad range of business reforms, including starting a business, obtaining access to electricity, registering property, protecting minority investors, and streamlining insolvency rules (Republic of Kenya, 2021c). Through the National Investment Policy,

Kenya aims to improve FDI by (a) modernizing FDI procedures; (b) assessing the effects of private investment at various levels of government; (c) making incentives available for foreign investors; and (d) furnishing a blueprint to augment investment by 32 percent of GDP by 2030 (Khawaja et al., 2020).

The Big 4 Agenda, an ambitious program launched to augment the Vision 2030 program, focuses on manufacturing growth, universal healthcare and affordable housing. It is considered to be a bold policy that will impact the economic development of the country. The program will help Kenya achieve faster investment growth to reach the Vision 2030 target of at least 32 percent of GDP. This will in turn, accelerate economic growth toward the double-digits, create jobs and enhance wealth. These kinds of big ideas are what will provide business opportunities to investors.

2.6.2 Public-Private Partnerships Program

A public-private partnership (PPP) is an arrangement under which a private party (a) performs a public function or provides a service on behalf of the public entity; (b) receives a benefit or compensation for performing the function; and (c) is generally liable for risks arising from performance (Republic of Kenya, 2021e). Current investment opportunities under Kenya's PPP policy are to be found in several sectors: transport and infrastructure; health solutions, including telemedicine; green and blue solutions, including water and sanitation; housing, including student hostels; industrial parks and manufacturing; ICT, including intelligent traffic management systems; airports; inland container depots and logistics hubs; petroleum infrastructure; ports; power generation plants and transmission/distribution networks; railways; roads and bridges; prisons; education; and solid waste management. Kenya's PPP policy framework is undergoing enhancements to scale up the legal and institutional frameworks in order to realize the full potential of PPP strategy.

2.6.3 Energy Sector Changes

Kenya's energy sector is among the most robust in Africa (Kenya Investment Authority 2021a). Energy is a vital resource and an imperative path to economic success in Kenya. As the economy is projected to grow, plenty of energy will be required to support this growth trajectory. Businesses also depend on the reliable and continuous availability of energy. Kenya continues to focus on improving energy availability to businesses and the general population (Khawaja et al., 2020). Significant legislative reforms have already been promulgated, creating a conducive environment for the private sector to participate in the development and supply of energy. More importantly, investors have the opportunity to invest in the energy sector by tapping into abundant solar, wind, biomass, and geothermal energy sources.

2.6.4 Agriculture

Agriculture remains the backbone of Kenya's economy, contributing one-third of GDP. About 70 percent of the country's exports are based in the agricultural sector. In 2020, growth in the sector was 6.3 percent (Republic of Kenya, 2021c). About 80 percent of Kenya's population of roughly 48.5 million work is at least part-time in this sector. Tea and coffee are the key exports, whose major markets are Europe, Africa, and Asia. Kenya is the world's third-largest exporter of cut flowers, and over 70 percent of the flowers are exported to Europe. Furthermore, Kenya's horticultural sector is the country's third-largest foreign exchange earner and contributes approximately 1 percent of the GDP. Kenyan fresh-cut flowers are sold in over 60 countries worldwide. Other agricultural products of economic significance include sugar cane, milk, maize, potatoes, bananas, milk products, cassava, sweet potatoes, macadamia, avocadoes, mangoes, guavas and cabbages. Investment opportunities in agriculture include production, processing, packaging, distribution and marketing, and logistical value chain support. To incentivize investment in agriculture, the government has scaled up the development and rehabilitation of irrigation schemes, credit and credit guarantees, supply of seed and fertilizer, and distribution and marketing, among others. Currently, agri-business attracts up to 20 percent of total FDI in the region, with prospects of growing further (Kenya Investment Authority, 2021c).

2.6.5 Tourism

Tourism also holds a significant place in Kenya's economy. As mentioned previously, the World Travel Awards ranked Kenya as the number one tourism destination in Africa. Despite this ranking, the tourism industry suffered a major blow with the onset of the COVID-19 pandemic, reporting a steep decline in the number of visitors and general tourist activity. To stimulate recovery, efforts are being made to promote aggressive post-pandemic tourism marketing, infrastructure development, financing and legal and institutional reforms. This will continue to provide an enabling environment for the sector to thrive and offer lucrative investment opportunities (Republic of Kenya, 2021c). Kenya is offering several propositions to investors, including financing, investing in new tourist circuits, development of resort cities, branding of premium parks, development of high-value niche products, building new high-end international hotels chains, developing innovation hubs, investing in African safaris, partaking in water and beach tourism, and development of cruise tourism and business tourism (Kenya Investment Authority, 2021c).

2.6.6 Products under the African Growth and Opportunity Act

Kenya is one of 39 Sub-Saharan African countries that currently enjoy duty-free export status to the United States for over 6,500 products through the African Growth and Opportunity Act (AGOA) and the US Generalized System of Preferences (African Growth and Opportunity Act, 2021). Through AGOA, Kenya benefits from preferential market access to the United States for various products, including textiles, clothing, motor vehicles and parts, many agricultural products, leather products, chemicals, wine, travel luggage, machinery and equipment. This provides a great opportunity for investors to tap into the US market for these products.

2.6.7 Kenyan Devolution System

As discussed under the *Structure of Government* in Chapters 1 and 4, Kenya's devolution decentralized government functions between the national and 47 county governments. It aims to increase citizen participation, foster inclusiveness, improve service delivery, and strengthen democracy. Furthermore, devolution seeks to promote social and economic development and provide proximate, easily accessible services throughout Kenya. County governments have negotiated a working relationship with the national government regarding power and revenue sharing. They have encountered political, fiscal, and administrative challenges in delivering services to Kenyans. Although the system of government is relatively new, it has shown significant strides in economic development in many rural areas. This model of government has the potential to spur faster economic growth at the county level by overcoming the bureaucracy of the previous centralized system. Counties have a profound impact on investments and business activity, and county governments can create investment opportunities for the private sector in practically all sectors of the economy. Furthermore, as consumers of various goods and services, county governments promote business opportunities.

2.7 Examples of Successful Industries

In 2020, Kenya's economy, like several others in the world, suffered from the consequences of the COVID-19 pandemic, affecting all sectors of the economy. Regardless, Kenya is still the leading economy in the region, with some industries reporting performance levels that would interest investors. The construction and real estate sectors are the fastest growing in Kenya, accounting for 5.7 percent of the GDP in 2019 (International Trade Administration, 2021). This growth is generally attributed to government investment in public infrastructure development projects (road, rail, energy, port and airport modernization) and real estate. The African Development Bank (2021) estimates that manufacturing accounts for only 9 percent of GDP and has remained stagnant for the past ten years. With the renewed focus on manufacturing through the Big 4 Agenda, this sector presents opportunities for investors.

As mentioned previously, agriculture is Kenya's economic mainstay, which, coupled with horticulture, constitutes the two largest sectors of the Kenyan economy (Food and Agriculture Organization, 2020). Kenya is the third largest producer and first exporter (in volume) of tea in the world. Kenya is also the ninth producer of dry beans, the 14th producer of oilseeds, and is among the 20 largest coffee exporters. In addition to tea, coffee, wheat, sugarcane, fruit, and vegetables are among the main crop exports, and dairy products, beef, fish, pork, poultry, and eggs, are the main animal products.

The tourism sector in Kenya is one of the most diverse in East Africa, with increased investments in conference, eco, and leisure tourism. The sector's prospects remain positive in the medium term, with a growth of 41 percent expected in 2021. This growth, coupled with investments in new hotel space and Kenya Airways' continued regional dominance, should keep the industry strong. Kenya is targeting 2.5 million visitors annually by 2024 and over three million by 2030.

The technology sector is also one of the fastest-growing business sectors in Kenya, and Internet access rates are some of the highest in sub-Saharan Africa. The enhancement of 4G and 4G LTE services in 2020, government-approved universal 4G coverage, and the rise in smartphone usage are influencing growth in the digital economy and other e-based services and innovation. Kenya has particularly distinguished itself in the services sector and has been the source of innovations adopted throughout the continent, including such financial technologies as M-pesa. In 2017, it became the first country to sell government bonds through telephone-supported technology.

Finally, although Kenya's mineral resources are limited, the country has an important source of high-value mineral commodities such as titanium, gold and rare earth minerals, and oil in Turkana (International Trade Administration, 2021). With the ongoing sector-specific and general business reforms, this sector has significant potential. Other sectors include textiles and apparel, food and beverages, paper, fishing, plastics, timber, pharmaceuticals, and energy.

2.8 Discussion

Stakeholders from Kenya's business environment and the government have recognized the value of economic development extended to the entire society's better quality of life when proper policies are implemented. While there has not been a total and universal application of business policy success, Kenya is progressing incrementally. As long as Kenya's political situation remains stable and there is an underlying desire to create business opportunities through entrepreneurship and business development, the country can continue down the path of positive economic possibilities. The list of successful business entities discussed above is testimony to the fact that business development is continuously possible on many fronts. It is the business community and sound government policies that will determine long-term outcomes.

The COVID-19 pandemic of 2020–2021 has impacted the entire world, causing significant turbulence in global trade. While Kenya has had its share of turmoil, it appears to be heading in the right direction. Hopefully, the next few years will see Kenya's economy experience double-digit growth. Two of the major areas that Kenyan businesses need to focus on are the issues of intellectual property and Internet access to businesses. Because the world in general, especially the business world, is so intricately connected with the Internet, it is imperative that Kenya's business developers, government policy makers, and future entrepreneurs concentrate on updating and implementing plans for installing state-of-the-art technology throughout Kenya. This is a major key to successful business development and economic growth.

2.9 Conclusion

Kenya's youthful population and skilled and educated labor pool are abundant positive factors for business development that bode well for its economic development. Compared to Kenya's neighbors, its infrastructure is superior and, in many cases, gets better over time. The Kenya Vision 2030 project rests on the pillars of economic, political, and social growth and development. Macroeconomic stability and infrastructure improvements, along with innovations in science and technology, are the key components that policymakers in both the private and public sectors must grapple with for Vision 2030 to succeed. If the Kenyan government and business leaders can fully operationalize the Vision 2030 principles and pillars, Kenya will have an extremely optimistic future. These observations conclude that Kenya is in a relatively good position to be open for investment.

References

Africa Regional Integration Index. (2021). Regional economic communities. Retrieved from https://www.integrate-africa.org/rankings/regional-economic-communities/

African Development Bank. (2021). Kenya economic outlook. Retrieved from https://www.afdb.org/en/countries-east-africa-kenya/kenya-economic-outlook

African Growth and Opportunity Act. (2021). Kenya's preferential market access to the United States. Retrieved from https://agoa.info/images/documents/15557/kenya-agoa-brochure-2021.pdf

Altman, A.S., and Bastian, P. (2021). The state of globalization in 2021. *Harvard Business Review*. Retrieved from https://hbr.org/2021/03/the-state-of-globalization-in-2021

Bellamy, M.W. (2020). Center for Strategic and International Studies. Retrieved from https://www.csis.org/analysis/kenyas-case-covid-19. Accessed May 1, 2021.

Center for Global Development. (2019). Digital technology and state capacity in Kenya. Retrieved from https://www.cgdev.org/publication/digital-technology-and-state-capacity-Kenya

Central Bank of Kenya. (2021a). Inflation rates. Retrieved from https://www.centralbank.go.ke/inflation-rates/

Central Bank of Kenya. (2021b). Bank supervision annual report 2019. https://www.centralbank.go.ke/reports/bank-supervision-and-banking-sector-reports/

Central Bank of Kenya. (2021c). The Kenya financial stability report. October 2020, Issue No. 11. Retrieved from https://www.centralbank.go.ke/u

Export Processing Zones Authority. (2021). EPZ program. Retrieved from https://epzakenya.com/

Food and Agriculture Organization. (2020). http://www.fao.org/kenya/programmes-and-projects/en/

Global Edge. (2020). https://globaledge.msu.edu/countries/kenya. Accessed September 2020.

Heritage Foundation. (2021). Index of Economic Freedom Kenya. Retrieved from https://www.heritage.org/index/?gclid=cj0kcqia6or_brc_arisapzuer9jy0t8_3syffmpb-9z8lzh1fp1whra9qlm1loejxc-

International Monetary Fund. (2020). *The African continental free trade area: Potential economic impact and challenges*. IMF. Retrieved from https://www.imf.org

International Monetary Fund. (2021). Kenya. IMF country report no. 21/72. *International Monetary Fund*. Washington, DC: Publication Services.

International Trade Administration. (2021). Kenya-country commercial guide. Retrieved from https://www.trade.gov/knowledge-product/kenya-market-overview

Kenya Airports Authority. (2021). Our airports. Retrieved from https://www.kaa.go.ke/

Kenya Association of Manufacturers. (2021). About KAM. Retrieved from https://kam.co.ke/

Kenya Bureau of Standards. (2021). About KEBS. Retrieved from https://www.kebs.org/index.php?option=com_content&view=article&id=6&Itemid=255

Kenya Investment Authority. (2021a). Investment Opportunities. Available from http://www.invest.go.ke/energy/

Kenya Investment Authority. (2021 About us. Retrieved from http://www.invest.go.ke/who-we-are/

Kenya Law. (2021a). The Constitution of Kenya, 2010. Kenya Law. Retrieved from http://kenyalaw.org/

Kenya Law. (2021b). Introduction to the Kenya law treaties and agreements database. Retrieved from http://kenyalaw.org/treaties/

Kenya National Bureau of Statistics. (2021). Economic survey 2021. Retrieved from https://www.knbs.or.ke/

Kenya National Chamber of Commerce and Industry. (2021). About KNCCI. Retrieved at https://www.kenyachamber.or.ke/

Kenya Private Sector Alliance. (2021). About KPSA. Retrieved from https://kepsa.or.ke/about-us/

Kenya Revenue Authority. (2020). Incentives for investors. Retrieved from https://www.kra.go.ke/en/ngos/

Kenya Vision 2030. (2020). The third medium term plan 2018-2022. Kenya Vision 2030. Retrieved from http://vision2030.go.ke/publication//

Khawaja, A., Wanjau, M.D., Mainnah, L., Nayfsa, A. and Okaalet, P. (2020). Doing business in 2020 chambers and partners. Retrieved from https://practiceguides.chambers.com/practice-guides/doing-business-in-2020/kenya/trends-and-developments. Accessed April 24, 2021.

Manda, D.K. and Sen, k. (2004). The labour market effects of globalization In Kenya. *Journal of International Development*. 16, 29–43. doi:10.1002/jid.1061

Mboya, E. (2020). Kenya overtakes Angola to become third-largest economy in Sub-Saharan Africa. *Business Daily*. https://www.businessdailyafrica.com/economy/Kenya-overtakes-Angola-as-third-largest-economy/3946234-5571578-ag2ukp/index.html

Naz, A. and Ahmad, E. (2018). Driving factors of globalization: An empirical analysis of the developed and developing countries. *Business & Economic Review*, 10(1), 133–158. doi:10.22547/BER/10.1.6

OECD Development Centre. (2003). Institutions and development: A critical review. Working Paper No. 210.

Peterson Institute for International Economics. (2018). What is globalization? Retrieved from https://www.piie.com/microsites/globalization/what-is-globalization.

Petryle, V. (2017). Does the Global Competitiveness Index demonstrate the resilience of countries to economic crises? *Ekonomika*, 95, 28. doi: 10.15388/Ekon.2016.3.10326.

Republic of Kenya. (2021a). Ease of doing business-reform milestones 2014-2020. *Ministry of East Africa Community & Regional Development*. Retrieved from https://kenyaembassydc.org/

Republic of Kenya. (2021b). Special Economic Zones Act 2015. Ministry of Industrialization. *Trade and Enterprise Development*. Retrieved from https://www.industrialization.go.ke/

Republic of Kenya. (2021c). 2021 budget policy statement. *The national treasury and planning*. Retrieved from https://www.treasury.go.ke/budget-policy-statement/

Republic of Kenya. (2021d). Mandate. Ministry of Industrialization, *Trade and Enterprise Development*. Retrieved from https://www.industrialization.go.ke/index.php/about-us/mandate

Republic of Kenya. (2021e). Private public partnership directorate. Retrieved from https://www.pppunit.go.ke/

Republic of Kenya. (2021f). Education sector report, medium term expenditure framework 2022/23-2024/25. Retrieved from https://www.treasury.go.ke/wp-content/uploads/2021/10/Education-Sector-Final-Report-13.10.2021.pdf

Republic of Kenya. (2021g). EAC achievements. Ministry of East African Community and Regional Development. Retrieved from https://meac.go.ke/eac-achievements/.

Republic of Kenya. (2021h). East Africa trading bloc ranked high in regional integration. *Ministry of Industrialization, Trade and Enterprise Development*. Retrieved from https://www.industrialization.go.ke/index.php/media-center/

Richman, M.B., and 1972). *International Management and Economic Development: With particular reference to India and other developing countries*. New York: McGraw-Hill.

The World Factbook. (2021). Explore all countries-Kenya. Retrieved from https://www.cia.gov/the-world-factbook/countries/kenya/#people-and-society

Transparency International. (2021). 2020 Corruption Perception Index. Retrieved from https://www.transparency.org/en

UNCTAD. (2016). UNCTAD XIV Outcome Nairobi Maafikiano and Nairobi Azimio. Retrieved from https://unctad.org/system/files/official-document/iss2016d1_en.pdf

US Department of Commerce. (2020). Keya commercial guide. International trade administration. Retrieved from https://www.privacyshield.gov/article?id=Kenya-Market-Overview

US Department of State. (2020). 2020 investment climate statements: Kenya. Retrieved from https://www.state.gov/reports/2020-investment-climate-statements/kenya/

Weimer, M.A. (1970). *Introduction to business: A management approach Hardcover*. Homewood, IL: Richard D Irwin, Inc.

World Bank. (2020). Doing business 2020: Economy profile Kenya. Retrieved from https://openknowledge.worldbank.org/bitstream/handle/10986/32436/9781464814402.pdf

World Bank. (2021a). Lower middle income. Retrieved from https://data.worldbank.org/country/XN

3 Kenya's Economic History, Legal System, Business Financing and Business Types

3.1 History of Kenya's Economic Performance

To gain a good understanding of the history of Kenya's economic performance, it is probably best to discuss the topic under distinct economic epochs. This is consistent with Nunn's contention that future work in economic history is to become more confined and specific in scope leading to inquiry into each growth episode (Nunn, 2009). According to Mwega and Ndu'ngu (2004), Kenya's economic development can be defined by different eras with varying degrees of performance. Therefore, for the benefit of our audience, the history of Kenya's economic performance is discussed under the following key periods: (a) the pre-colonial era (before 1895), (b) the colonial era (between 1895 and 1960), the 1960s–1970s, the 1980s–2002 and 2003 to present.

3.1.1 The Pre-Colonial Era

a   The Economy during the Pre-Colonial Era

Early communities that settled in the part of East Africa that is now called the nation-state of Kenya, lived as independent units within the boundaries of their areas of habitation (Ochieng & Maxon, 1992). These societies consisted of many small competing ethnic groups, often feuding over natural resources such as land, water, pasture, and boundaries. Furthermore, they were fragmented and isolated, often with porous territorial boundaries. Inter-community interactions were characterized by trade, intermarriage, and intermittent warfare.

These communities focused on agricultural production, animal keeping, and some forms of rudimentary processing, while others leaned toward hunting and gathering (Green, 2013). Other activities were mining and basic manufacturing. Production was mainly for the communities' self-sustenance, with little or none for commerce. Ownership of factors of production, which included land, livestock, and labor vested in the community.

Most of the trade in pre-colonial Kenya, just like the rest of Africa, was not with countries beyond the continent but consisted of the local exchange. Trade with the outside world was non-existent except for a few

DOI: 10.4324/9781003095156-3

Arab and European traders who ventured into the interior, introducing new commodities, which they exchanged with the local people for slaves, ivory, and other goods. Local trade was generally highly organized, and the exchange of goods and services was facilitated through barter trade for the most part but later metamorphosed into a monetized economy. Communities rarely leveraged their comparative advantages on a commercial scale. Inter-community and/or external trade involved prestigious goods whose impact on the communities was minimal. The surplus was quantitatively negligible, thus militating against trade and commerce (Green, 2013).

An insufficient supply of human resources was a major limitation to production, which curtailed extensive agriculture (Ochieng & Maxon, 1992). Family members and neighbors often pooled to supply the necessary labor to tend the land and build other community-based amenities. Furthermore, mechanized and modern farming practices were non-existent, thus curtailing the full potential of agricultural production. Efficient and effective strategies lacked to control adverse weather conditions leaving the farmers at the mercy of Mother Nature.

The traditional economic phase changed dramatically with the advent of the colonial administration and the arrival of immigrant communities, which introduced capitalism and a cash economy. Soon, Kenya's indigenous communities assimilated and adopted the newly introduced economic ideas and practices, most of which define current Kenya's economic landscape. It is worth noting that most of the institutions introduced by the colonial administration were to play an important role in the transformation and development of markets in the postcolonial period.

b   *The arrival of the Arabs*

This is a watershed period during which early transboundary commercial activities and trade emerged by the first century AD when Arab traders frequented the Kenyan coast. Around the seventh century, Arabs, Indians, Persians, and even Chinese arrived on the Kenyan coast to trade skins, ivory, gold, and spices. It was during this period that the Swahili language developed as a lingua franca for trade between different peoples. Arab dominance on the coast was eclipsed by the arrival of the Portuguese in 1498. The Portuguese built Fort Jesus in 1593, which today is one of Mombasa's top tourist attractions. By 1730 all the Portuguese had left the East African coast, paving the way to Islamic control under the Imam of Oman in the 1600s until the 1800s when the British came along.

3.1.2 Colonial Period (1895–1963)

Britain governed Kenya between 1895 and 1963, first as a protectorate and later as a colony (Ochieng & Maxon, 1992). The Imperial British East Africa Company, the forerunner of the British colonial administration, took over the long-distance trade that linked the African interior to the African coast and the African coast to the Indian subcontinent via the Indian Ocean. To enhance the profitability of the coast and the hinterland route, the British built a railway from Mombasa to Kampala using Indian laborers. Major cities and towns were founded along the railway line, backed by European settler farming communities.

White settlers moved increasingly into the fertile hinterlands and introduced large-scale farming. Many Asians (mainly Indians) arrived during this period and later established shops in the newly established urban centers. The European settler farming community and the Indian shopkeepers established the foundations of the modern formal Kenyan economy.

Kenya's current economic system, particularly certain key institutions, is derived from the British colonial administration, as aforementioned. As Nunn (2009) noted that Acemoglu et al. (2001), La Porta et al. (1997, 1998) and Sokoloff and Engerman (2000) in their research acknowledged the important role of institutions play in economic development and how *"historical events can be an important determinant of the evolution and long-term persistence of domestic institutions"* (p. 67). As elaborated in Chapter 5, several of Kenya's economic institutions originated in the colonial era, including the Central Bank of Kenya, the Nairobi Securities Exchange, Kenya Revenue Authority and the National Social security Fund.

3.1.3   Post-Colonial Era (1960s to-date)

a   *Between 1963 and 1970s*

The 1960s and 1970s, except for 1975 to 1979, were a period of economic prosperity; the economy recorded an average growth rate of about 6 percent (Mwega and Ndungu, 2004). Kenya's GDP grew at an annual average of 6.6 percent from 1963 to 1973 and 7.2 percent during the 1970s. It is instructive that Kenya's meteoric performance in the 1960s slightly surpassed the High Performing Asia Economies by about 0.10 percent. Between 1975 and 1979, the economy deteriorated to an average growth rate of 5.2 percent due to failed policies compounded by the oil price shocks, which led to an unfavorable balance of payments.

Soon after independence in 1963, Kenya was to serve mainly as a source of raw materials for British industries and a market for their products. As a former British colony, it was natural for Kenya to mimic the development strategies of the western economies, ostensibly Britain. Kenya adopted policies that emphasized entrepreneurship and capital accumulation as critical twin agents of growth. The government applied the second agent by unleashing massive capital to foster the formation of strong market links, which spurred economic development. The resultant growth was driven by public investment, smallholder agricultural production, and incentives for private, often foreign industrial investment.

Agriculture made a significant contribution to economic growth during this period, probably because of what some economists have described as favorable policy conditions (Bates, 1989). Among the policies attributed to the strong performance in agriculture is the expansion of the farming area; allowing African farmers to participate in cash crop production; improved agricultural productivity because of new technologies; reform in land management policy including private ownership; efficient exchange rate management; and support by agricultural parastatals (Lofchie, 1989). Meanwhile, the manufacturing output, bolstered by the policy of import substitution strategy, grew fairly fast. However, due to inadequate capacity in the economy and the inherent policy weaknesses, the import protection and import substitution strategies did not satisfy the domestic demand and eliminate imports as anticipated.

Between 1974 and 1990, Kenya's economic performance declined. GDP growth averaged 4.2 percent in the 1980s and 2.2 percent in the 1990s (Kaimenyi et al., 2016). This state of affairs is attributed to run-away inflation and declining growth rates, which led to subdued growth across all sectors. To compound the problem, the value of Kenya's exports fell drastically. A combination of these adverse economic conditions, together with poor weather conditions, impacted Kenya's terms of trade and balance of trade negatively.

How did the government respond? The government implemented a raft of policies, including sweeping measures targeting the private sector. Some of the measures introduced include (a) selective controls on bank lending, (b) licensing of foreign exchange transactions; (c) quota restrictions on most imports; (d) direct price controls on goods; and (e) control on interest rates. However, the lack of export incentives, tight import controls, and foreign exchange controls made the domestic environment for investment even less attractive. These controls did not yield much success; rather, they inhibited the development of markets, constraining resource movements and efficient allocations and, thus, growth.

b   *The 1980–2002 Epoch*

The 1980s and 1990s, except from 1985 to 1989, represented a period of dismal economic performance (Kaimenyi et al., 2016). The 1980s have been regarded as a lost decade for growth by some economists. The main factors attributed to this performance are the impact of the second oil price shock in 1979, a military coup attempt in 1982, and a severe drought in 1983/1984. A brief interlude spanning 1985 to 1989 saw Kenya's poorly performing economy reverse and record some growth (averaging 5 percent per annum). This period is associated with a mini coffee boom, a decrease in oil prices, and good weather.

The first half of the 1990s represented a challenging economic environment, with a low growth rate of 2.5 percent. It was during this period that Kenya reported the worst economic performance since independence due to drought, a sharp increase in oil prices, an aid embargo, and social disruptions. Kenya also witnessed a significant increase in the budget deficit and money supply leading to uncontrolled inflation and exchange rate depreciation, liberalization of the foreign exchange market, and other unfavorable conditions.

How did Kenya address the aforementioned economic challenges? Kenya sought resources attached with austerity conditions from the Bretton Wood Institutions (International Monetary Fund and The World Bank), paving the way to remarkable donor-driven reforms under the auspices of the structural adjustment programs in the 1980s and 1990s. The reforms covered a wide range of sectors of the economy, including the liberalization of the foreign exchange market, trade, and payments system; domestic financial and capital markets; and privatization of public enterprises. However, these reforms did not produce the intended results, rather, they contributed to further economic decline and a two-decade stagnation of the economy.

c   *The 2003–2020s Epoch*

Between 2003 and 2008, economic growth improved following an ambitious economic reform program and the resumption of cooperation with the World Bank and the International Monetary Fund. Real GDP grew from 2.8 percent in 2003 to 7.0 percent in 2007. However, growth decelerated to less than 2.3 percent in 2008 due to a variety of reasons.

Between 2009 and 2018, growth returned to an average of 5 percent. Despite this growth, Kenya's debt sustainability, current account deficit, fiscal consolidation, and revenue growth were major concerns. By 2019, Kenya's economic growth averaged 5.7 percent, making Kenya one of the fastest-growing economies in Sub-Saharan Africa. This growth trajectory is attributed to a stable macroeconomic environment, positive investor confidence, and a resilient services sector (World Bank, 2020) driven by strategies anchored in a major policy blueprint, Vision 2030 Third Medium Plan, in which the government aims to create a prosperous, and globally competitive nation with a high quality of life by the year 2030 (Kenya Vision 2030, 2020). Furthermore, in 2017 to rationalize the country's priorities in Vision 2030, President Uhuru Kenyatta introduced the 'Big Four Agenda,' covering manufacturing, universal healthcare, affordable housing and food security, as key development priority areas (Republic of Kenya, 2020a). President William Ruto, elected in August 2022, campaigned on a "bottom up economic model "comprised of six pillars. These six pillars are: Agriculture; Micro, Small and Medium Enterprise (MSME) economy; Housing and Settlement; Healthcare; Digital superhighway and creative economy; Environment and climate change.The new government has begun work on these six pillars whose primary goal is to improve the lives of the ordinary Kenyan citizen (Mwananchi).

3.2 Kenya's Legal Environment

3.2.1 Introduction

In this section, we analyze Kenya's legal environment highlighting the salient business laws and institutions that impact business. To demonstrate the criticality of law in business, imagine attempting to do business where you do not have reasonable expectations of other people's behavior. In the same vein, visualize a situation where investors conduct business without the legal means to protect their property interests. Furthermore, imagine if organizations can invest in innovation and research and development where legal mechanisms for protecting intellectual property rights are lacking. In the absence of law, how would contracts be enforced? Without a credible legal system that is predictable, objective, efficient and fair, resolving disputes would be a nightmare, let alone the erosion of confidence to invest and conduct business on credit terms that may ensue.

To address the abovementioned concerns, an efficient, effective, and predictable legal system is required to inspire confidence in investors. The reality is that in a globalized economy, goods and services, and investments move across borders, which invariably subject businesses to the complexity of regulation and liability in other countries (Cox, 2016).

Law applies to businesses just the same way as people. As it relates to business, the law prescribes business types and their formation, defines business policies, provides investment incentives, and regulates business practices, including rights and obligations involved in a business transaction. Laws will also aim to regulate chemicals, limit air and water pollution, protect property rights, control the impact of computer technology and cyber security, and govern bankruptcy and governance.

A business can do most things that a person can do, and laws are necessary to control those activities. It can also buy and sell property, sue and be sued, enter into contracts, hire and fire employees, and even commit crimes. Furthermore, every business is bound to comply with the relevant laws, including laws relating to business formation, taxation, the level of competition and antitrust, consumer protection, employment, health and safety, the environment and nature, business ethics, as well as court structures. For this reason, investors need a clear understanding of the legal environment, whether domestic or foreign, in which they operate to help them make informed decisions.

A legal system impacts the investment environment of a country. If the legal system is too rigid, the economy is likely to be restricted, thus curtailing business activity. Indeed, La Porta et al. (1997, 1998) argued that countries with legal systems based on British common law offer greater investor protection than countries with legal systems based on civil law. Therefore, countries with a common law tradition will likely be viewed as better investment destinations than civil law-oriented countries.

3.2.2 Kenya's Legal System

Kenya's legal system is a hybrid of English common law, Islamic law and customary law (Kenya Law, 2021a). It embeds the 'western' style free market models, including private ownership of business enterprises. The elements of Kenya's legal system comprise the constitution, statutory laws, common law, principles of equity and customary law. The constitution is the supreme law of the land and takes precedence over all other forms of law, written or unwritten (Kenya Law, 2021b). Kenya's new constitution of 2010 has resulted in significant legal reforms in different aspects of public administration and economic management.

Most of Kenya's laws are based on English statutes on similar subjects with modifications where it is deemed necessary. African customary law and Islamic law may be applied in personal matters (e.g., marriage, divorce, succession), provided that it does not contradict any statutory law and is not offensive to justice and morality. Common law fills voids left by the constitution and statutory laws. Most of the common law in Kenya is based on English common law and equitable principles.

To encourage private investment and competition, the constitution guarantees the sanctity of private property for all people, citizens and non-citizens (Kenya Law, 2021b). Therefore, the state cannot appropriate the property or investment of any person without compensation. Furthermore, the Foreign Investments Protection Act makes it unlawful for the government to expropriate private property (Kenya Law 2018, 2011; Nairobi Securities Exchange 2021). Kenya has no history of expropriating foreign investments.

3.2.3 Application of the Law

The judiciary, one of three branches of government, is responsible for interpreting the constitution and adjudicating disputes or controversies which arise out of the laws (Kenya Law, 2021b). The judiciary consists of five superior courts made up of the supreme court, the court of appeals, the high court, the industrial court, the environment, and the land court. The subordinate courts are made up of the magistrate's courts, courts–martial and Kadhi's Court (Kenya Law, 2021b). The supreme court, the highest court of the land, has both original and appellate jurisdiction, and its decisions are binding on the court of appeal, the high court, the magistrate's courts, as well as specialized courts and tribunals.

To enforce contracts more efficiently, Kenya introduced a case management system for commercial dispute resolution. Effective and efficient resolution of commercial disputes encourages new business relationships, and promotes speedy trials, which saves businesses valuable time and high litigation costs. From position 149 in 2012, Kenya ranked number 89 in 2020 in enforcing contracts (World Bank, 2020). This indicator measures the time and cost of resolving a commercial dispute, the quality of judicial processes, and the adoption of good practices that promote quality and efficiency in the court system.

Is international law relevant in Kenya? The Constitution of Kenya recognizes international law as part of the domestic legal order. In 1965, Kenya accepted the compulsory jurisdiction of the International Court of Justice with reservations (International Court of Justice, 2021). Kenya ratified the Rome Statute in 2005, effectively enabling the International Court of Justice to exercise its jurisdiction over Kenya or its nationals. This would provide further comfort and confidence to foreign investors in Kenya.

However, Kenya's legal recourse is not flawless. It has been indicted as slow and expensive and somewhat replete with subjectivity in certain executive and judicial branch decisions (U.S. Department of State, 2021). Recent reforms in the general business legal environment and the judicial system above address these challenges. Almost in all legal indicators for Kenya, a considerable improvement has been recorded.

Finally, a discussion of a legal system would be incomplete without a mention of the lawyers in practice. A good legal system needs not only an effective and efficient bench but also an active and professional bar.

Kenya has a robust body of lawyers comprising about 17,000 duly qualified members who practice in different specialties and branches, including commercial law, conveyancing, criminal law, family law, environmental law, intellectual property law, constitutional law, international law, and labor law (Law Society of Kenya, 2021).

3.2.4 Alternative Dispute Resolution

In Kenya, litigation is the traditional method of resolving disputes. However, recent developments have seen alternative dispute resolution (ADR) methods such as mediation, arbitration, conciliation and negotiation gain traction. ADR offers several advantages, including the opportunity for the parties to use a single procedure, thereby avoiding the expense and complexity of multi-jurisdictional litigation and the risk of inconsistent results (World Intellectual Property Organization, 2020). ADR allows parties to exercise greater control over how their dispute is resolved than the case in court litigation. Unlike court decisions, which can generally be contested through one or more rounds of litigation, arbitral awards are not normally subject to appeal.

To strengthen ADR, Kenya's Constitution and several laws encourage the use of ADR as a method of resolving disputes. Kenya is a signatory to the United Nations Convention for the Recognition and Enforcement of Foreign Arbitral Awards of 1958, known as the New York Convention (Kenya Law, 1971), and has adopted the United Nations Commission on International Trade Law model of arbitration. The New York Convention generally provides for recognizing arbitral awards on par with domestic court judgments without review of the merits. This greatly facilitates the enforcement of awards across borders.

There is also an active local chapter of the Chartered Institute of Arbitrators (Kenya Law, 1995). Most commercial contracts contain arbitration clauses making arbitration the first option for resolving commercial disputes. Rarely do courts interfere with arbitration proceedings or contradict determinations arising from the arbitration. Increasingly, mediation and negotiation are also becoming preferred approaches for commercial dispute resolution.

3.3 Forms of Business Organization

3.3.1 *Types of Business in Kenya*

Business types may be differentiated by their respective cost structures and the products they sell to their customers. Major business types are service, merchandising, and manufacturing. A fourth type, called hybrid, combines any two or more of the three types above of business. All four business types are to be found in Kenya.

a   *Service Business*

Service businesses are those firms that sell services instead of physical products to their customers (Cheeseman, 2016). Service-type firms offer professional skills, expertise, advice, and other similar products, including accounting, law, marketing, banking, consultancy, healthcare, communications, hospitality, education, and training.

One major difference between service companies and merchandising and manufacturing firms is that service companies do not have the cost of goods sold because there is no product being sold. Service firms also do not have inventory, also because no physical product is being sold. There may be direct costs associated with providing the service, but no physical product.

As East Africa's distribution hub, telecommunications axis and financial center, Kenya has a broad array of well-developed services industries. Examples of service companies in Kenya include Kenya Airways, Kenya Commercial Bank, Strathmore University and Deloitte.

b   *Merchandising Business*

In merchandising business, the company sells products, also known as merchandise but does not make the products (Cheeseman, 2016). Merchandisers purchase merchandise or inventory and sell it to customers without changing their form. When inventory is sold, the cost of that inventory is called the cost of goods sold, an expense that is charged in the income statement of the business. Merchandising firms are broken up into two different types: retailers and wholesalers. Retailers sell products directly to the end user. They sell products that consumers and businesses use rather than resell. Wholesalers buy products from manufacturers and sell them to other merchandising companies, usually retailers. These distributors have established relationships with local outlets, making it easier for manufacturers to get their products to the market. Wholesalers are sometimes referred to as "middlemen" because they act as an intermediary between a manufacturer and a retailer. In Kenya, such firms as Niavas and Chandarana are examples of merchandisers.

c   *Manufacturing Business*

A manufacturer makes a product using labor and machinery, and raw materials (Cheeseman, 2016). New KCC Ltd., Dell Computers and General Motors are manufacturers. While some manufacturers sell their products directly to the end user, others sell their products directly to consumers and to retailers. In Kenya, manufacturers make several types of products, including foods and beverages, chemicals, apparel and footwear, motor vehicles, machinery, cement, steel, and rubber (Kenya National Bureau of Statistics, 2020).

d   *Hybrid Business*

Hybrid businesses may be classified into more than one type of business (Cheeseman, 2016). Some businesses sell both merchandise and services to customers. A restaurant, for example, combines ingredients in making a fine meal (manufacturing), sells a cold bottle of wine (merchandising) and fills customer orders (service). A fitness center is another example of one such business. Patrons of the gym buy a membership and go there to work out on machines, take fitness classes and work with a trainer – all of which are services the fitness center provides. But visitors can also purchase workout accessories such as weights and clothing to enhance the workout experience. Good examples of hybrid businesses in Kenya include the Hilton Hotel.

3.3.2 Forms of Business Organization

It is critically important for an investor to understand the different forms of business as this will help to structure and plan for the business entity accordingly. The main forms of business organizations in Kenya are (a) sole proprietorships, (b) partnerships, (c) limited liability partnerships, (d) companies, (e) branch offices of a foreign registered company and (f) cooperative societies and state-owned enterprises (BDO, 2021).

a   *Sole Proprietorship*

A sole proprietorship, also known as a sole trader or a proprietorship, is often described as the simplest form of business that one can operate

(Cheeseman, 2016). It is an unincorporated entity with a single owner who manages the business and pays personal income tax on profits earned from the business. Many sole proprietors do business under their names. Furthermore, a sole proprietorship is the simplest, most common type of business, and the least costly business to form. It normally operates as a first business before transitioning to other business types.

A sole proprietor assumes all the business risks with no limit to his or her investment in the business. Apart from the business owner, no one else has the authority to make any binding decisions regarding the business. Furthermore, sole proprietorships, unlike companies, face restrictions to access funds, which are generally limited to personal resources and loans. The business ceases with the death of the owners or transfer.

In Kenya, sole proprietorships are registered as provided by the Registration of Business Names Act (Kenya Law, 2017a). The proprietorship business will need to apply for name approval, pay the prescribed fees and attach the prescribed documentation to complete the application process. If the application is deemed appropriate, a certificate of registration is issued to the applicant by the Registrar.

b   *Partnership*

A general partnership, or simply partnership, is a business owned by two or more persons who voluntarily contribute resources to form a business organization with the objective of carrying on a business, trade, or profession and sharing in profits (Cheeseman, 2016). It is a corporate body that can sue and be sued, capable of entering into contracts and holding property (Kenya Law, 2012).

Partnerships pull together more than one person's expertise and other resources, thus reducing the chances of business failure. Each partner contributes their skills, money, or property to have a share in the business so that they can share in the losses and profits of the business. In addition, the formalities of registration (cost, requirements, duration) are minimal, making it an attractive business structure. The partners share the profits and losses of the business among themselves.

The partnership is liable for any acts caused by a partner, employee or agent within the ordinary course of business, and each partner is jointly and severally liable for torts and breaches of trust (Kenya Law, 2012). Partners are jointly liable for the partnership's contracts; no one partner can be held responsible for contracts assumed by the business.

Its formation requires little or no formality, and ordinary partnerships can operate under the name of any one or more of the partners or a fictitious name. The partnership business will need to apply for name approval and pay the prescribed fees, documentation, and particulars in the prescribed manner to secure registration (Kenya Law 2017a).

c   *Limited Liability Partnership*

A limited liability partnership is a unique business association comprising at least two and up to twenty persons coming together to carry on a business with a profit-making motive. It is a corporate body that can sue and be sued, capable of entering into contracts and holding property. At least one member should be a general partner who should be liable for all debts and obligations of the firm. Furthermore, one or more persons should be a limited partner whose liability is limited to the amount so contributed (Kenya Law, 2011).

A natural person or a corporate body may be a partner in a limited liability partnership, and the limited liability partnership must have a manager who must reside in Kenya. The mutual rights and duties of the partners, and those of a limited liability partnership and its partners, are governed by a partnership agreement or the Limited Liability Partnership Act.

The setting of a limited liability partnership business is similar to the aforementioned general partnership business. It can operate under the name of any of the partners or a fictitious name. Furthermore, it needs to register its employees with NHIF and NSSF (Kenya Law, 2019).

d   *Companies*

A company is a business organization with a separate legal personality distinct and independent from its owners (Kenya Law, 2019). Accordingly, a company can own property, execute contracts, raise debt, make investments and assume other rights and obligations independent of its members. A company can also sue and be sued on its name as a legal entity. Lastly, the most striking consequence of separate legal personality is that a company survives the death of its members. Shares of stock represent ownership in a company.

The shareholders are normally removed from the day-to-day management of the company but appoint boards of directors to run the business. The boards of directors normally delegate the responsibility or manage the business to professional management teams whose members might not be company owners. Different types of companies are found in Kenya including statutory companies and registered companies, and a discussion of these types of companies is as follows.

e   *Statutory Companies*

A statutory company is incorporated through legislation made by Parliament to create the company to operate according to commercial principles. Such a company has no shareholders, and the government provides its initial capital. If it cannot pay its debts, theoretically, its property can be attached by its creditors unless the government steps in to pay the creditors. Examples of statutory companies include Kenya Broadcasting

Corporation, Industrial and Commercial Development Corporation, and Kenya Ports Authority (State Corporations Advisory Committee, 2021).

f   *Registered Companies in Kenya*

Registered companies are classified into three broad categories. First, in terms of the extent to which the members are exposed to the company's debts in the event of liquidation, thus, limited or unlimited liability companies' classification (Kenya Law, 2019). Second, the source of the assets for paying the members' liability for a limited company in liquidation. Where the assets have been transferred to the company, we have a company limited by shares, and where the assets are with shareholders, it is a company limited by guarantee. The next category is based on the company's ability or restriction to raise investment funds from the public, viz. private or public companies. Finally, is classified according to the country of formation. If incorporated in Kenya, we have a local/domestic company, and if formed outside Kenya, it is a foreign company.

Both private and public companies are either limited or unlimited liability companies. Only limited liability public companies can be limited by guarantee or shares. Limited liability private companies, on the other hand, are limited only by shares. Foreign companies may assume any one or more of the forms of companies described in this section.

3.3.2.1 *Limited Companies*

In a limited company, the liability of the members or shareholders is limited to the amount of their investment or guarantee in the company (Kenya Law, 2019). Whereas the company has rights and obligations of its own and a life separate from its owners, the shareholders bear responsibility and liability to the extent of their shareholding in the company. As a general rule, shareholders will be liable only to the extent of their capital contributions and not personally liable, for the debts and obligations of the company. Examples of limited liability companies in Kenya include East African Breweries and Safaricom Ltd. (Office of Attorney General and Department of Justice, 2021).

3.3.2.2 *Unlimited Companies*

In an unlimited company, the liability of its members, is not limited to their investment in the company (Kenya Law, 2019). The company's shareholders are individually and jointly responsible for the debts and other liabilities of the company, regardless of how much capital each contributes. The shareholders are compelled to use their assets to settle the company's debts if it fails financially.

3.3.2.3 Companies Limited by Shares

Shares limit a company if the liability of its members is limited to the unpaid amount on the shares held by the members (Kenya Law, 2019). Suppose the company cannot pay its debts and obligations when they are due. In that case, the creditors cannot recover the money owed by the company from the shareholders beyond the shareholders' investment in the company. Examples of companies limited by shares include Safaricom, Kenya Commercial Bank, East African Breweries, and KenGen Ltd. (Office of Attorney General and Department of Justice, 2021a).

3.3.2.4 Companies Limited by Guarantee

A company limited by guarantee (a) does not have a share capital, and (b) the liability of its members is limited to the amount that the members undertake to contribute to the assets of the company in the event of its liquidation (Kenya Law, 2019). The members' exposure to the company's debts is limited to the members' undertaking to support the company.

3.3.2.5 Private Companies

A limited liability private company is a legal entity owned by a few in-dividuals that are closed to the public. Furthermore, it restricts a member's right to transfer shares, limits the number of members to at least one and no more than 50, and it prohibits invitations to the public to subscribe for shares or debentures of the company (Kenya Law, 2019). Examples of private companies in Kenya are Sony Sugar Co. Ltd., Family Bank Ltd. and Thwama Building Services Ltd.

3.3.2.6 Public Companies

A public limited liability company has shares owned by diverse public members of an unlimited number (Kenya Law, 2019). The public can buy and sell shares in the company. Furthermore, its shares may be traded in the stock/securities market. In Kenya, a public company shares are traded at either the first-tier or second-tier markets the Nairobi Securities Exchange (NSE). Examples of companies whose shares are traded at the NSE include Equity Bank Ltd. Safaricom Ltd, East African Breweries Ltd. (Nairobi Securities Exchange, 2020).

3.3.2.7 Foreign Company

A foreign company may conduct business in Kenya by registering either a branch office or a subsidiary in Kenya (Kenya Law, 2019). A subsidiary is a company that is controlled or owned by another company but stands on its own as a separate legal entity. Moreover, a subsidiary is considered a local company with compliance requirements similar to those of local companies owned by Kenyan investors. To be a subsidiary in Kenya, majority ownership of the subsidiary must vest in another company, or the directorship/membership of the subsidiary should be controlled by the holding company. A branch office, on the other hand, is an extension of the operations of a foreign company. As such, it relies on the direction of the leadership of the foreign company for making decisions.

g   *Registration of Companies*

Registering a company in Kenya is governed by the Companies Act (Kenya Law, 2019) and the associated regulations. As part of the registration process, the company must obtain registration with NSSF, NHIF, and KRA (Office of Attorney General and Department of Justice, 2021a). Depending on the business type, a business permit should also be obtained from the County Government.

The applicant must initiate the registration process by lodging a set of prescribed documents with the Registrar through the e-citizen platform, an online gateway to government information and services. The first step is to apply for approval of the company's business name. Furthermore, articles of association for the company should be provided together with the application. These are a set of internal regulations that govern the day-to-day operations of the company, and they are the rules and regulations of the company. They deal with the rights of the company members among themselves (Kenya Law, 2019).

Objects of the company showing the primary and secondary activities of the company must be indicated on the application form. The objects section states the purpose and range of activities for which the company will engage. If exceeded, the company may be cited for acting *ultra vires* (beyond its legal powers) and may attract sanctions or render actions under such powers unactionable.

In Kenya, the company's memorandum of association is treated as part of its articles. The main purpose of the memorandum of association in Kenya is to demonstrate that subscribers are willing to form a company and agree to become members of the company (Kenya Law, 201). In other countries such as the United Kingdom and the United States, the memorandum contains the name of the company, object clauses, authorized share capital, and the full particulars of the initial subscribers of the company. Company registration documents have been exempted from stamp duty eliminating the requirement for stamp duty.

h   *Registration of a Branch of an Overseas Registered Company*

The registration process of a branch entails setting up an e-citizen account and submitting to the Registrar the parent company's registration documents, including copies of the company's constitution and certificate of incorporation issued by the company's home country (Office of Attorney General and Department of Justice, 2021a). It may be necessary to supply additional information to complete the registration process.

Payment of the prescribed fee should be made, following which the Register issues a certificate of compliance (Kenya Law, 2019). The foreign company is then expected to apply for company and directors' (KRA) Personal Identification Number (PIN), National Social Security Fund (NSSF) employee registration, and National Health Insurance Fund (NHIF) employee registration. Upon satisfying the registration conditions, the Registrar shall sign the certificate for the foreign company and authenticate it.

i   *Cooperative Societies*

A cooperative society may be defined as "*a people-centered enterprise owned, controlled, and run by and for its members to realize their common economic, social, and cultural needs and aspirations*" (International Cooperative Alliance, 2021, p. 1). In Kenya formation of cooperative societies is governed by the Co-operative Societies Act (Kenya Law, 2017b) and the SACCO Society Act (Kenya Law, 2018a) together with the corresponding rules and regulations. Cooperatives are bodies corporate with perpetual succession and with the power to hold movable and immovable property, to enter into contracts, to sue and be sued, and to do all things as permitted by their by-laws (Kenya Law, 2017b).

The liabilities of the members are limited to the extent of their capital contributions in cooperative societies. Unlike companies, cooperative societies are exempt from income tax. Besides, they are also exempted from stamp duty and registration fees. Management of the cooperative societies is entrusted to management committees elected by the entire membership.

Compared to other business organizations, cooperatives are relatively easy to establish. Any ten adults can join together and form a cooperative society (Kenya Law, 2017b). An application for the registration of a society is made to the Commissioner of Societies in the prescribed manner, accompanied by an appraisal of the viability of the society and payment of the prescribed fee. Examples of SACCOs include Cooperative Insurance Company, Afya SACCO, Ardhi SACCO, Kenya USA Diaspora SACCO, New KCC Ltd. and Stima SACCO (Sacco Societies Regulatory Authority 2021).

Initially, predominantly rooted in the agricultural sector, however, in the recent past, the cooperative movement in Kenya has engendered diversified economic activities and interests, notably savings and credit, housing, transport and small-scale industries. This sector is a key player in the economy, controlling about 43 percent of Kenya's GDP (Kenya National Bureau of Statistics, 2020). Kenya's SACCO sector is one of the largest in Africa, with a 5.7 percent of total assets to GDP ratio (International Cooperative Alliance, 2021).

It is worth noting that several cooperatives lack the business acumen and professional management skills necessary to run the cooperatives efficiently. This is exacerbated by the fact that management committees are constituted exclusively from the general membership, which may not necessarily possess the requisite capacity. Furthermore, given that cooperatives are not motivated by profits may create an environment of laxity and complacency and pursuit of goals that are anything but profitability. However, the SACCO regulator, SACCO Societies Regulatory Authority, has instituted measures through regulations and education geared to strengthen the sector.

j   State-Owned Enterprises

State-owned enterprises (SOEs) are businesses where the national or subnational government has significant control through full or majority ownership, also called state corporations (International Monetary Fund, 2020). According to the Presidential Taskforce on Parastatal Reforms, an SOE is an *"entity, howsoever incorporated, that is solely or majority owned by the government or its agent for commercial purposes"* (State Corporation's Advisory Committee, 2013, p. 144). In Kenya, the minority owners of SOEs may be citizens of Kenya and/or non-citizens. Examples of SOEs owned jointly by the Kenya government and foreign investors include Agro-Chemical and Food Companies, Pan African Paper Mills, Kenya Petroleum Refineries and some sugar companies.

SOEs are to be found in virtually every country worldwide and are among the largest corporations in some advanced economies, and constitute at least one-third of the largest firms in several emerging markets. In Africa and Asia, SOEs dominate power generation. Kenya's 35-odd SOEs are no exception; they traverse practically all sectors of the economy (State Corporation's Advisory Committee, 2021), and they are intended to serve as vehicles for social and economic development. They are also expected to create a market for goods and services from other sectors, contribute to the accumulation of foreign exchange through exports, attract FDI and technology transfer, supply goods and services, create employment, pay taxes and dividends to the government, and support other sectors to grow.

To revamp SOEs and realign their functions to the national development goals, the Kenya government has instituted several reforms, including privatization, liberalization, and private-public partnerships. Other reforms are structural changes and policy reorientation. To illustrate an SOE reform, in 2020, the executive reorganized the management of Kenya Ports Authority, Kenya Railways Corporation, and Kenya Pipeline Company and mandated the Industrial and Commercial Development Corporation to oversee rail, pipeline, and port operations through a holding company called Kenya Transport and Logistics Network (the Republic of Kenya, 2020c).

3.4 Business Financing in Kenya

3.4.1 Financing Theory

Corporate or business financing is perhaps one of the most critical functions that preoccupy business managers throughout the life cycle of the business. It is the act or process of raising or providing funds for business activities, making purchases, or investing (Damodaran, 2010). Different businesses have different financial needs, usually dictated by the type and size of the business. While some businesses may require large amounts of capital, others may only need a smaller portion. Whatever the needs are, business financing falls into two categories, debt, and equity. Debt is borrowed money, and equity constitutes funds provided by the business owners.

We now turn our attention to two theories of finance which seem to complement each other. According to the firm value maximization theory, financing decisions seek to maximize revenues which ultimately increase returns for shareholders (Culata & Gunarsih, 2012). In other words, a business will select financing or a mix of different financing forms with the prospects of the highest possible returns. The pecking-order theory states that internal financing is preferred to external financing, and when external financing is required, firms should issue debt first and equity last (Majluf & Stewart, 1984). This theory is predicated on the premise that there is an asymmetry of information between business internal stakeholders and external financing providers, which impacts the cost of financing. The proponents of this theory posit that business managers are more likely to comply with the following pecking order of financing: own finance (retained earnings), non-risky debt, risky debt and lastly, equity (from additional investors). In Kenya, businesses appear to follow the pecking-order theory for their financing needs.

For the most part, businesses in Kenya are funded with a mix of debt and equity. Grants and/or guarantees from the government and other organizations are yet another source of business finance. Moreover, investment incentives such as tax holidays discussed in Chapter 2 are a form of indirect financing, are often availed for businesses to set up their operations in certain areas and/or encourage activities in particular industries (Republic of Kenya, 2020b). For publicly traded firms, debt may take the form of bonds and equity (preferred stock). For private businesses, debt is more likely to be bank loans while an owner's savings represent equity. According to the Kenya Investment Authority (2021a), all of these forms of finance are available in Kenya with varying degrees of access. Some are more easily available, while others are not.

3.4.2 Equity Financing

Equity represents the owners' capital contribution to a business venture (Agarwal, 2009). Equity financing is the process of raising capital from current and potential owners of the business. While equity financing normally refers to the financing of public companies listed on an exchange, it also applies to private company financing. Equity involves a permanent investment in a business and is not required to be repaid by the firm at a later date. In the next section, we discuss how a firm may raise equity capital.

3.4.2.1 Initial Public Offering

Equity capital can be raised through the sale of shares or stocks of a company in return for cash, through initial public offerings (IPOs), and/or rights issues. IPO is the process of offering shares of a private company to the public in a new stock issuance through a stock exchange for the first time (Capital Markets Authority, 2020a), thereby allowing the issuing company to raise capital from public investors. It is a very complex, time-consuming, and expensive process involving many actors, including transaction advisors, accountants, lawyers, investment banks, investors, promoters, stock brokers, underwriters and regulators. However, it is an attractive method and a viable source of raising business financing.

The effect of equity financing is that a portion of the ownership of the business is traded for financial investment in the business (Hofstrand, 2013). The firm's cash flow increases from equity financing while control by pre-equity investment owners is diluted as additional investors join the business. In Kenya, IPOs are conducted through the NSE, which is regulated by the Capital Markets Authority (Kenya Law, 2018b).

A rights issue, on the other hand, is an invitation to existing shareholders to purchase additional new shares in the company. This type of issue gives existing shareholders securities called *rights*. With the *rights*, the shareholder can purchase new shares at a discount to the market price on a stated future date.

In Kenya, companies such as Safaricom Ltd., KenGen Ltd., Co-operative Bank of Kenya, and British American Ltd. have raised substantial amounts of capital through IPOs (Nairobi Securities Exchange, 2021a). Some companies that have utilized the rights issues route are Kenya Commercial Bank, Housing Finance Corporation, Kenya Airways and Kenya Commercial Bank.

3.4.2.2 Retained Earnings

Retained earnings are the undistributed profits of a business usually reported as part of the general reserves of the business. The amount of retained earnings will typically depend on the level of profits earned, dividend payments, taxation, etc. Retention of earnings is an internal source of financing, which does not involve floatation costs and the uncertainties of external financing. The main disadvantages of retained earnings financing are that these earnings are fully dependent on the accuracy of profits and the possibility of improper use of funds by the management. Many businesses in Kenya plow back part of their profits into the business for expansion and/or modernization.

3.4.2.3 Personal Savings or Bootstrapping

For many private businesses for example sole proprietorships, family-owned firms, and partnerships, the key source of equity financing is the investors' savings or bootstrapping. The first place to look for money for business is your savings. Personal resources include salaries and wages, profit earrings or early retirement funds, or cash value insurance policies. Equity financing can also be obtained by selling part of the business to potential partners. It can also be obtained by selling part of the investors' property, like land.

3.4.2.4 Family and Friends

Another popular source of equity financing for private enterprises is support from the investor's family and friends. This could be in form of debt capital at a low-interest rate that is lent to the investor to invest in the business. Another equally popular source of equity capital is self-organized groups, also called *chamas*. These groups serve as vehicles for saving, lending, and borrowing money for a section of the population that does not access formal financial systems. *Chamas* is based on close social ties and is highly dependent on trust. In addition, such *chamas* offer members financial and social support.

3.4.2.5 Savings and Credit Cooperatives

Obtaining loans/credit from Savings and Credit Cooperatives (SACCOs) is much simpler and less costly compared to banks. Terms and conditions of borrowing from SACCOs are less stringent, members can guarantee one another thus dispensing with the traditional collaterals that bank demand. SACCOs also charge lower interest rates than banks. In addition to loans, SACCO members also earn dividend and interest income from their SACCOs which they can use as equity capital.

3.4.2.6 Microfinance and Digital Lenders

Microfinance or microcredit refers to the financial services provided to low-income individuals or groups who are generally excluded from traditional banking and formal financial services. Borrowing from microfinance institutions is less demanding than banks. Most of these institutions focus on offering credit through small working capital loans, sometimes called microloans or microcredit. However, many also provide insurance and money transfers, and regulated microfinance banks provide savings accounts. Through the Microfinance Act, the Central Bank of Kenya licenses and regulates deposit-taking microfinance institutions (MFIs). Examples of MFIs in Kenya include Caritas, Faulu Kenya, Kenya Women, and Century (Central Bank of Kenya, 2020). Non-deposit-taking microfinance institutions are regulated by the Ministry of Finance and are not allowed to mobilize public funds. Thus, they can only lend their funds or borrowed funds.

Digital financial institutions also provide a rich source of financing which supply loans instantly since loan-eligibility decisions are automated based on a predetermined criterion formulated on available data. Another distinguishing feature of digital credit is that information, loan disbursements, and repayments are managed remotely. Owing to the high-cost funds, and to mitigate the risk of loan repayment default, microfinance and digital lenders offer their loans at higher rates of interest than commercial banks. Examples of digital lenders in Kenya include Mshwari, Equity Eazzy, and KCB M-Pesa (Central Bank of Kenya, 2021).

3.4.2.7 Private Equity

Private equity investors invest, and acquire equity ownership, in private companies, typically those in high-growth stages. These equity funds purchase shares of private companies or those of public companies that go private, with a strategy to exit later. Private equity firms may assume either a passive or active role in the portfolio company. Passive involvement is common with mature companies with proven business models that need capital to expand or restructure their operations, enter new markets or finance an acquisition. Active involvement, on the other hand, means that the firm plays a direct role in restructuring the company.

While venture capital is a subset of private equity, there is a difference between the two. The most notable difference is that venture capital funds raise capital from investors to specifically invest in startups and small- and medium-sized private companies with strong growth potential. Some examples of private equity funds in Kenya include Catalyst Principal Partners, Savannah Fund, and FSD Africa (Capital Markets Authority, 2021).

3.4.2.8 Venture Capital

Venture capital is risk financing invested normally in young private businesses with high growth prospects, with not less than 75 percent of the funds consisting of equity or quasi-equity investment in qualifying enterprises (Kenya Law, 2018b). In Kenya, venture capital is regulated by the Capital Markets Authority. It is emerging as a popular source of financing for businesses that generally do not have adequate capacity to access funds from more traditional sources, such as public capital markets or banks.

Venture capital firms also prefer businesses with a competitive advantage or a strong value proposition, demonstrated demand for the product or service, or a novel idea or innovation with high commercial value. The number of venture firms has increased significantly over the years, consistent with the economy. Some of the leading venture capital firms in

Kenya are Novastar Ventures Ltd., Safaricom's Spark Fund and Viktoria Ventures (Capital Markets Authority, 2021).

Venture capitalists are sometimes characterized as angel investors or vulture investors. Angel investors typically focus on earlier-stage financing and smaller financing amounts than venture capitalists. These are usually wealthy individuals that come together in investor networks and can provide capital in exchange for a portion of equity. A vulture investor is a type of venture investor who specifically looks for opportunities to make money by buying poorly run or distressed firms for example firms with high-yield bonds in or near default or equities that are in or near bankruptcy.

3.4.3 Debt Financing

Debt capital is financing from creditors, normally financial institutions, with the condition of repaying the borrowed funds (principal) plus interest at a specified future date. The lender (creditor), earns interest as the reward for the amount lent to the borrower.

We now focus on the common types of debt. Debt may be secured or unsecured. Secured debt has collateral, normally a valuable asset that the lender can attach to satisfy the debt if the debtor defaults on repayment. Unsecured debt, on the other hand, does not have collateral and exposes the lender to the risk of default. Debt may also be characterized as short-term or long-term in its repayment schedule. Generally, short-term debt is used to finance current activities such as operations, while long-term debt is used to finance assets such as buildings and equipment. In Kenya, in addition to security, most banks require viable business plans and a positive track record for a borrower to access bank credit.

Kenya has an extensive and relatively well-established banking industry, serving domestic and regional markets. There are about 44 banks registered in the country (Central Bank of Kenya, 2021). They include household names such as Barclays and Standard Chartered, indigenous commercial banks such as Kenya Commercial Bank and Diamond Trust Bank, and others that evolved from a cooperative movement orientation such as Equity Bank and the Co-operative Bank. The larger banks have built a strong business in servicing the regional operations of local and foreign companies operating in Kenya.

In addition to commercial banks, development financial institutions (DFIs) provide long-term credit to businesses. DFIs are usually majority-owned by national governments, and they source their capital from national or international development funds or benefit from government guarantees. The main bilateral DFIs include AFD/Proparco (France), KfW/DEG (Germany), CDC Group (United Kingdom), and OPIC (United States). Examples of multilateral DFIs are the African Development Bank, East African Development Bank, Trade and Development Bank (previously, PTA Bank),

European Investment Bank, International Finance Corporation, and Islamic Development Bank.

Kenyan DFIs include the Agricultural Development Corporation, Kenya Industrial Estates, Agricultural Finance Corporation, Development Finance Company of Kenya, Industrial Development Bank, Industrial and Commercial Development Corporation, and Tourism Finance Corporation. These institutions typically impose less rigorous conditions for lending compared to commercial banks. However, they control fewer resources as they depend on government appropriations.

3.4.4 Bonds and Commercial Paper

A bond is a debt instrument in which an investor lends money to an entity (bond issuer) for a defined period at a variable or fixed interest rate. Bonds are used by companies, municipalities, states, and sovereign governments to raise money and finance a variety of projects and activities. Bonds may be used to raise financing for specific activities. They are a special type of debt financing because the issuer issues the debt instrument. The bond issuer specifies the interest rate and when the principal will be paid back (maturity date).

Corporate bonds are long-term (at least one year and above) debt instruments issued by the private sector as opposed to treasury bonds issued by governments. Issuers of these instruments target institutions and high net worth and sophisticated investors. Treasury bonds are medium to long-term debt instruments, usually, longer than one year, issued by the government to raise funds in local currency to supplement government revenue from other sources.

Another debt instrument commonly used to raise capital is commercial paper. The main difference between a corporate bond and a commercial paper is that the former is usually used for raising long-term credit. In contrast, the latter is predominantly relevant for short-term, usually less than one year, to fund requirements such as working capital.

Whereas bonds and commercial papers are issued to the public through stock exchanges, they may also be issued privately through private placement. Unlike a public offering, a private placement is subject to less regulation and information disclosure. A private placement allows the issuer to sell more complex security to accredited investors like fund managers who understand the potential risks and rewards. The buyer of a private placement bond issue expects a higher rate of interest than can be earned on a publicly traded security.

Examples of fund managers involved with bonds and commercial paper operating in Kenya include Britam Asset Managers, Old Mutual Investment Group, and Cytonn Asset Managers (Capital Markets Authority, 2021). It is not unusual for firms in Kenya to engage in more than one type of business financing service. Some companies raising financing through corporate bonds in Kenya are Stanbic Bank, Commercial Bank of Africa, East Africa Breweries Ltd., and Family Bank.

3.4.5 Derivatives

A derivative is a financial instrument whose value is derived from the value of one or more underlying assets, including equity, commodity, currency or bond (Nairobi Securities Exchange, 2021b) where two parties agree to payoffs based upon the value of the underlying asset or other data at a particular point in time. Derivatives may be broadly classified into four categories, forwards, futures, options, and swaps, currently (Nairobi Securities Exchange, 2021b).

A futures contract, the only derivative currently traded on the NSE, is a standardized agreement made through an exchange to buy or sell an asset at a future date, at a pre-determined price in the future. The forces of demand and supply determine prices as the contracts are traded on an organized exchange. Futures contracts require either physical delivery of the asset or settlement in cash.

On the other hand, a forward contract is a non-standardized contract between two parties to buy or sell an asset at a specified later date, at a price agreed at the time of signing the contract (Nairobi Securities Exchange, 2021b). An options contract entitles the holder of the contract to buy or sell the asset underlying the option at a pre-determined price during or at the end of a specified period. A swap is a private agreement between two parties to exchange one financial instrument for another in the future according to a prearranged formula. The exchange takes place at a pre-determined time, as defined in the contract.

Some examples of recent derivate contracts in Kenya include Safaricom Ltd., Kenya Commercial Bank Group, Equity Bank, East Africa Breweries Ltd., Equity Bank and Absa Bank Ltd. (Capital Markets Authority, 2020b).

3.4.6 Leasing

A lease is a legal agreement for the rental use of a tangible asset such as a building and equipment. The agreement usually involves the lessee (party using the asset), the lessor (the owner of the asset) and sometimes a leasing or financing organization (intermediary). It facilitates the use of an asset without using debt or equity financing. The lessee pays the lessor rent for the use of the leased asset. When the lease ends, the asset is returned to the owner (lessor), the lease is renewed, or the lessee purchases the asset. An advantage associated with a lease is that it does not tie up funds from purchasing an asset and that lease payments often come at the beginning of the year. Examples of leasing companies in Kenya are Vehicle and Equipment Leasing Limited, Rentco East Africa Limited, NIC Leasing LLP, Simba Corporation, and Ryce East Africa Corporation.

3.4.7 Trade Credit

Trade credit can be defined as a contract between the buyer and the seller/supplier for procurement of goods or services where delivery of the goods or services and payment thereof do not occur simultaneously. One version of trade credit is where delivery precedes payment of the purchase price. The buyer takes possession and assumes ownership of the goods before paying for them. In such an arrangement, the buyer is the debtor, while the seller is the creditor. Trade credit may also occur when the buyer pays the supplier for later delivery. In such a case, the seller becomes the debtor and the buyer the creditor.

The terms of the credit will depend on several factors, including credit worthiness of the debtor, the financial strength of the creditor, the purchase price, and the duration of the credit. A debtor with a better credit rating is more likely to secure better credit terms than one with a weaker rating. A creditor firm with a stronger financial base is likely to provide softer credit terms than one struggling. Some trade credit contracts may involve a cash discount, while others may not. The discount serves as a motivation for early payment. In Kenya, trade credit is a popular source of financing, particularly for manufacturing, wholesale, and retail businesses, as well as public and private bulk procurement.

3.4.8 Invoice Factoring

Invoice factoring is a form of business financing through which a receivable (invoice) holder sells for immediate cash the receivable to a third party, called the 'factor,' and the factor takes over the receivable and collects the debts from the customer (the debtor). In this transaction, the factor becomes the creditor and assumes the credit risks of the factored invoices. Factoring eliminates the credit period on the invoice and provides a firm with the funds it needs to run its business. Factoring is a common business financing practice in Kenya. Some of the factoring companies in Kenya include Kenya Commercial Bank and Equity Bank.

3.4.9 Grants

A grant may be defined as money or product given by a government, organization or person (grantor or grantmaker) to a recipient (grantee) for a specific purpose (Cambridge, 2020). Usually, to receive a grant, recipients are required to submit proposals or applications to the grantmaker. Unlike loans, grants are not paid back to the grantor. However, grants must be used for the purpose they are given.

In Kenya, grants for business financing are normally provided to vulnerable members of society, including the youth, women, persons with disabilities, and small businesses. They are also commonly used to support businesses hurting due to adverse economic conditions. In 2020, many businesses globally received grants from their governments during the Covid-19 pandemic.

The Kenya government, on its own or jointly with bilateral and multilateral agencies or private sector organizations, may provide such grants. Individuals and private sector institutions are also major sources of grants for business activities. Examples of organizations that pride Kenyan businesses include the World Bank, United States Agency for International Development, Canadian International Development Agency, Norwegian Agency for Development Cooperation, Mastercard Foundation, Coca-Cola Foundation, Safaricom Foundation, Melinda Gates Foundation, etc.

3.4.10 Guarantees

A guarantee is a promise or undertaking by the surety, also called a guarantor to be responsible for the debt or obligations of the principal debtor made to the debtor's creditor (Legal Dictionary, 2021). The debtor is not privy to the guarantee, and the guarantor is not a party to the principal obligation. A guarantee creates a latent or conditional obligation and becomes operative only when the principal debtor is in default. It imposes an obligation upon the surety and crystalizes only when the borrower (the debtor) fails to repay the debt.

A loan guarantee serves as additional protection against the risk of default, making the loan more attractive to potential lenders. The lenders are more willing to provide guaranteed loans even to candidates with a poor credit profile, as the presence of a guarantee diminishes the probability of the loan repayment default. The guarantor's promise may allow borrowers to obtain loans that would otherwise be inaccessible.

Three basic guarantees are commonly available: personal, bank, and government guarantees. A personal guarantee is a promise made by an individual to repay liabilities on behalf of another individual or organization. On the other hand, a bank guarantee is a promise from a bank to cover the liabilities of a debtor in case the debtor fails to fulfill contractual obligations with another party. Commercial banks or specialized insurance companies usually provide it to companies involved in international trade with unfamiliar parties or foreigners. The third type of guarantee covered is a government guarantee which is a "*form of the sovereign obligation described as binding or potentially binding in a written document to satisfy certain obligations of an underlying contract, or to protect the beneficiary from defined losses if specified conditions occur*" (World Bank, 2019, p. 1). Government guarantees are commonly used where commercial guarantee by the private sector is either too costly or simply not available.

The Kenya government has provided partial risk guarantees through letters of support and indemnity agreements to bilateral and multilateral agencies to secure capital for organizations as Kenya Power and Lighting

Plc and Geothermal Development Corporation to meet their obligations. Furthermore, from time to time, the government appropriates funds in the form of guarantee funds to cushion lenders against potential losses of credit repayment delinquency by beneficiary borrowers as a means of promoting certain policies. For example, in 2016, through an agricultural credit agreement, the Kenya government guaranteed credit of KES 300 Million by Equity Bank to farmers under the auspices of the Kilimo Biashara Partnership (Equity Bank, 2016). Furthermore, in 2017, the government offered a guarantee to cover debts owed by Kenya Airways, a public company, to the US Exim Bank and local lenders as a reprieve for the heavily indebted carrier securing financing from other sources to complete its recovery (Reuters, 2017).

3.5 Discussion

Kenya's economic development has evolved from the traditional systems of subsistence farming and barter trade to a modern, complex monetized economy. The trajectory of Kenya's economic growth rate has been anything but a consistent trend. It has been cyclical, rising to a high of 7.6 percent and a low of negative 1 percent. The prosperous periods are characterized by well-formulated economic goals and sound strategies, good weather, and favorable global economic conditions. The periods associated with poor performance, on the other hand, show poor economic management exemplified by price control, protection of local industries, regulated exchange rate regime, low FDI inflows, adverse weather conditions, adverse global economic phenomena like uncontrolled oil prices, global recession, international financial crises, depreciation of the local currency against major international currencies and weak fiscal and monetary policies.

Although Kenya's macroeconomic outlook has been described as strong, some challenges abound, key among them being poverty, inequality, climate change, continued weak private sector investment, and the economy's vulnerability to internal and external shocks. Furthermore, unemployment remains fairly high, and manufacturing, agriculture, and the labor market are likely to be subdued in the face of the Coronavirus pandemic.

Effective legal system functions encourage investment, both local and foreign, compared to systems that are opaque, slow, and costly. Competitive countries generally have legal systems that provide a strong mechanism for setting up and enforcing contracts. Inefficient contract mechanisms increase the cost of doing business. Although Kenya's judiciary is generally independent, courts are undermined by weak institutional capacity and systemic inefficiencies.

Several forms of business organizations are similar to those in many other capitalistic economies in Kenya. However, the majority of these businesses are small to medium size firms, mainly sole proprietorships. The small size undermines the businesses' ability to access business financing. Policymakers will need to implement policies that facilitate such firms to access financing or support them to transition to more stable forms of business. The business registration has improved significantly, placing Kenya in an enviable position in the region and the world.

Kenya has a robust financial system that facilitates business financing. Different forms of debt and equity capital are available, including loans, debentures, trade credit, personal savings, bootstrapping, equity capital, venture capital, and grants. However, it is critical to enhancing capacity in the financial services to provide adequate capital deepening. In the same vein, CBK and other relevant institutions must ensure adequate security against financial risks, threats and other vulnerabilities, particularly, those emanating from the Internet.

3.6 Conclusion

The cyclical nature of Kenya's economic growth is not unique; every economy experiences similar variability over different time horizons. However, the gist of the matter is how well Kenya manages its economy with sound strategies likely to yield a strong economy, thereby making Kenya a more attractive investment destination. It may be remembered that the global financial meltdown of 2009 and the COVID-19 pandemic in 2020 impacted all countries to varying degrees. Lessons learned from such past episodes are important because they help policymakers, and investors to prepare better for the future and hopefully avoid any prior missteps. For Kenya to achieve high growth will depend on improved economic governance and greater economic reform to improve the country's investment climate.

The inefficiencies noted in Kenya's judicial system will need to be addressed through appropriate legal and institutional reforms. As pointed out above, countries with legal systems that are perceived as inefficient are unlikely to inspire investors. We contend that close collaboration with investors in any reform agenda envisaged will benefit all concerned.

Lastly, many businesses lack adequate financing for various reasons, including lack of collateral and ability to issue securities. To improve access to business financing, facilitative reforms may be necessary. Moreover, experience from countries that have demonstrated success in business financing may be adopted in Kenya, among other measures.

References

Acemoglu, D., Simon, J., and James, A.R. (2001). The Colonial Origins of Comparative Development: An Empirical Investigation, *American Economic Review*, 91(5), 1369–1401. 10.1257/aer.91.5.1369

Agarwal, O.P. (2009). *Corporate Financial Policy,* Himalaya Publishing House. ISBN: 978-93-5202-357-8

Bates, R.H. (1989). *Beyond the Miracle of the Market: The Political Economy of Agrarian Development in Kenya*, Cambridge: Cambridge University Press, 1989

BDO (2021). *Types of Business Entities*. https://www.bdo-ea.com/en-gb/

Cambridge Dictionary (2020). *Grant*. https://dictionary.cambridge.org/us/

Capital Market Authority (2020a). *Initial Public Offering. Capital Markets Authority*. https://www.cma.or.ke

Capital Markets Authority (2020b). *Quarterly Statistical Bulletin Issue 44/2020*. https://www.cma.or.ke/

Capital Markets Authority (2021). List of Licensees March 2021. https://www.cma.or.ke/

Central Bank of Kenya (2020). *Licensed Microfinance Banks*. https://www.surveyscentralbank.go.ke/

Central Bank of Kenya (2021). *The Kenya Financial Stability Report*. October 2020, Issue No. 11. https://www.centralbank.go.ke/u

Cheeseman, H.R.Z. (2016). *The Legal Environment of Business: Online Commerce, Business Ethics, and Global Issues*, 8th ed., Upper Saddle River, NJ: Pearson Prentice Hall. Textbook/Component. ISBN: 9780133973310

Cox, N. (2016). *Technology and Legal Systems*, New York: Routledge. ISBN 9780754645443.

Culata, P., and Gunarsih, T. (2012). Pecking Order Theory and Trade-Off Theory of Capital Structure: Evidence from Indonesian Stock Exchange, *The Winners*, 13, 40. 10.21512/tw.v13i1.666.

Damodaran, A. (2010). *Applied Corporate Finance*, 3rd ed., New York: University Stern School of Business. http://pages.stern.nyu.edu/

Equity Bank (2016). Government of the Republic of Kenya & Equity Bank Sign Credit Guarantee Scheme (ACGS) Agreement. https://equitygroupholdings.com/g

Green, E. (2013). Production Systems in Pre-colonial Africa. In E. Frankema, E. Hillbom, U. Kufakurinani and F.M. Selhausen (Eds.), *The History of African Development: An Online Textbook for a New Generation of African Students and Teachers*, African Economic History Network

Hofstrand, D. (2013) *Types and Sources of Financing for Start-up Businesses*. https://www.extension.iastate.edu/agdm/wholefarm/pdf/c5-92.pdf

International Cooperative Alliance (2021). *What Is a Cooperative Society?* https://www.ica.coop/en/cooperatives/cooperative-identity

International Court of Justice (2021). *Declarations Recognizing the Jurisdiction of the Court as Compulsory*. https://www.icj-cij.org/en/declarations/ke

International Monetary Fund (2020). *State-Owned Enterprises*. https://www.imf.org

Kaimenyi, M.S., Njuguna, N.S., and Mwega, F.M. (2016). *The African Lions: Kenya's Case Study*, Washington, D.C.: The Brookings Institution.

Kenya Investment Authority (2021a). *Our Services*. http://www.invest.go.ke/

Kenya Law (1971). *Convention on the Recognition and Enforcement of Foreign Judgments in Civil and Commercial Matters*. http://kenyalaw.org/treaties/

Kenya Law (1995). Arbitration Act, *Kenya Law*. http://kenyalaw.org

Kenya Law (2011). *The Limited Liability Patronship Act*. http://www.kenyalaw.org/lex/rest//db/kenyalex/

Kenya Law (2012). *Partnerships Act*. http://kenyalaw.org:8181/exist/kenyalex/

Kenya Law (2017a). *Registration of Business Names Act*. http://www.kenyalaw.org/lex//

Kenya Law. (2017b). *Cooperatives Societies Act*. http://www.kenyalaw.org

Kenya Law (2018a). *Sacco Societies Act*. http://www.kenyalaw.org:8181/

Kenya Law (2018b). *Capital Markets Act.* http://www.kenyalaw.org:8181/

Kenya Law (2019). *Companies Act.* http://www.kenyalaw.org:8181/exist/

Kenya Law (2021a). What is Law Reporting? *Kenya Law.* http://kenyalaw.org/kl/

Kenya Law (2021b). *The Constitution of Kenya, 2010.* http://kenyalaw.org/

Kenya National Bureau of Statistics (2020). *Economic Survey 2020.* https://www.knbs.or.ke/

Kenya Vision 2030 (2020). The Third Medium Term Plan 2018-2022. Kenya Vision 2030. http://vision2030.go.ke/publication//

La Porta, R., Lopez-de-Silanes, F., Shleifer, A., and Vishny, R. (1998). Law and Finance, *Journal of Political Economics*, 106, 1113–1155

Law Society of Kenya (2021). *Introducing LSK.* https://lsk.or.ke/about-lsk/

Legal Dictionary (2021). *Guarantee.* https://legal-dictionary.thefreedictionary.com/

Lofchie, M.F. (1989) The Policy Factor: Agricultural Performance in Kenya and Tanzania (Food in Africa Series). Lynne Rienner Pub; 1st US - 1st Printing edition (January 1, 1989). ISBN-10: 1555871364

Majluf, N.S., and Stewart, C.M. (1984). Corporate Financing and Investment Decisions When Firms Have Information That Investors Do Not Have, *Journal of Financial Economics*, 13(2), 1984, 187–221.

Mwega, F. and Ndungu, N. (2004) Explaining African Economic Growth Performance: The Case of Kenya. *ARC.* https://pdfs.semanticscholar.org/

Nairobi Securities Exchange (2021a). *Company Announcements.* https://www.nse.co.ke/

Nairobi Securities Exchange (2021b). *NSE Derivatives Market.* https://www.nse.co.ke/derivativefaq.html

Nairobi Securities Exchange (2020). *Listed Companies.* https://www.nse.co.ke/

Nunn, N. (2009). The Importance of History for Economic Development, *The Annual Review of Economics.* 050708.143336.

Ochieng, W.R., and Maxon, R.M. (1992). *An Economic History of Kenya.* Westlands, Nairobi: East African Educational Publishers Ltd. ISBN. 9966-46-963-X.

Office of Attorney General and Department of Justice (2021). Incorporation of Companies. https://brs.go.ke/company-incorporation.php

Republic of Kenya (2020a). Speech by His Excellency Hon Uhuru Kenyatta, During the 2017 Jamhuri Day Celebrations. *The Presidency.* https://www.president.go.ke/2017/12/12//

Republic of Kenya (2020b). Ease of Doing Business-Reform Milestones 2014-2020. *Ministry of East Africa Community& Regional Development.* https://kenyaembassydc.org/

Republic of Kenya (2020c). The Executive Order Establishing Kenya Transport and Logistics Network. *The Presidency.* https://www.president.go.ke/2020/08/07/

Reuters (2017). Kenya government to guarantee $750 mln in Kenya Airways debt. https://jp.reuters.com/article/

Sacco Societies Regulatory Authority (2021). Licensed Saccos. https://www.sasra.go.ke/

Sokoloff, K.L., and Engerman, S.L. (2000). Institutions, Factor Endowments, and Paths of Development in the New World, *Journal of Economic Perspectives, American Economic Association*, 14(3), 217–232, Summer.

State Corporations Advisory Committee (2013). *Presidential Taskforce on Parastatal Reforms.* https://www.scac.go.ke/

State Corporations Advisory Committee (2021). Commercial and Manufacturing State Corporations. https://www.scac.go.ke

U.S. Department of State (2021). *Investment Climate Statements: Kenya.* https://www.state.gov/reports/2021-investment-climate-statements/kenya/

US. International Development Corporation (2021). *Investing in Development.* https://www.dfc.gov/

World Bank (2019). Government Guarantees for Mobilizing Private Investment in Infrastructure. *International Bank for Reconstruction and Development,* 2019.

World Bank (2020). *Doing Business 2020: Economy Profile Kenya.* https://openknowledge.worldbank.org/

World Intellectual Property Organization (2020). *ADR Advantages.* https://www.wipo.int/amc/en/center/advantages.html

4 The Political Climate in Kenya

4.1 Introduction

This chapter discusses Kenya's political landscape and system of government as key aspects of business investment. Political instability significantly increases the risk quotient towards discouraging any business investment. Political instability significantly increases risk and discourages business investment. In 2021, large geographic areas became off-limits to many business ventures even though they had an abundance of valuable natural resources. For example, Venezuela is ranked number one in the world with the largest oil reserves of any country on the globe (World Population Review, 2022). Yet, the continued political turmoil that exists in that country discourages business investment.

Similarly, in Africa, the Central African Republic is a perfect example of a country that is well endowed with uranium, crude oil, gold, diamonds, and other natural resources. Yet, it is ranked as one of the poorest countries in the world, with a GDP per capita of $900 in 2020 (CIA Factbook, 2021). Additionally, places such as Syria, Afghanistan, Somalia, Congo, Nigeria, and some other countries have presented political and governance arrangements that are not attractive to business development. When governments such as Russia and Iran are subject to intense restrictions caused by the imposition of external political sanctions, they become undesirable for investment even though both countries have extensive factors of endowment that many investors would love to own and use in their business enterprises. Throughout the world in contemporary 2021, we have seen large geographic areas become off-limits to many business ventures. Issues of business nationalization, expropriation and insecurity emerge as negative terms in the eyes of business investors.

4.2 Background

Kenya acquired independence from Great Britain in 1963, and in 1964 Kenya became a member of the British Commonwealth. During this transition period, Kenya adopted a Westminster model with a multiparty

DOI: 10.4324/9781003095156-4

republican system of government (Kanyingi, 2014). Kenya comprised several political parties, including the Kenya African National Union (KANU) and the Kenya African Democratic Union (KADU) and Jomo Kenyatta, the leader of KANU, became Kenya's first prime minister. Soon after, the first government dismantled the multiparty system making Kenya a *de facto* single political state, namely, KANU, and concentrated power in the executive through constitutional amendments. In 1982, under President Daniel Arap Moi, parliament changed the constitution to make Kenya a *dejure* one-party state. During the one-party rule, democratic space was drastically constrained. Nonetheless, elections were held regularly, as was then provided for in the constitution. The country remained under a one-party system until 1991 when the constitution was amended to provide a return of multiparty democracy.

By 1997, 26 political parties were registered in Kenya, 10 of which had representatives in parliament. Further constitutional amendments were made to allow for more rights and freedoms. Owing to certain weaknesses in the prior constitution, the 2010 constitution was passed, and at the time, it was lauded as the most progressive constitution in Africa. The new 2010 constitution introduced several institutional and legal reforms and resulted in a devolved government (Kenya Law, 2021a). Since 2003, Kenya has had three presidents, Mwai Kibaki (2003–2012) and Uhuru Kenyatta (2013–2022). President William Ruto was elected as Kenya's 5th president in August 2022 for a five year term. Political tensions flared up during national elections, calling for further debates on creating a more secure and united country. However, Kenya has successfully held elections every five years as required by law since independence, albeit characterized by ethnic tensions. During national elections, political tensions are usually high; therefore, companies doing business in Kenya must prepare for potential violence during the election cycle.

4.3 System of Government

Kenya has a multiparty political system, which is well known for its parliamentary democracy. Under the 2010 constitution, Kenya is a unitary state divided into 47 counties (i.e., semi-autonomous subnational entities) (Kenya Law, 2021a), creating two levels of government, the national government, and the county government. The primary objective of decentralization was to devolve power, resources, and representation down to the local level to unlock the country's economic potential through distributing responsibilities.

Consequently, the government consists of the executive branch, the judicial branch, the legislative branch and the devolved government (counties). The constitution requires the national government to share revenue with the county governments. The counties may raise their revenues, such as fees.

4.3.1 Executive

The executive branch comprises the president, deputy presidentthe deputy president, and the cabinet secretaries (Kenya Law, 2021a). The constitution requires that Kenya have elections for the president, parliament, and local authorities every five years.

The executive implements and administers public policy enacted by the legislature, and its authority is vested in the president, the head of the state, and the government. The cabinet aids and advises the president. Cabinet secretaries, appointed by the president, exercise control over ministries.

4.3.2 Legislative

The legislative branch is a bicameral house consisting of the National Assembly and the Senate, whose members are elected and nominated during the general elections to represent citizens (Kenya Law, 2021a). Duties and responsibilities of the legislature include making laws, approving the appropriation of public finances, controlling and overseeing public expenditure, vetting candidates for appointment to certain public offices, and checking on the two other branches of government.

4.3.3 Judicial

The judicial branch adjudicates disputes and interprets the constitution (Kenya Law, 2021a). The judiciary of Kenya consists of five superior courts made up of the Supreme Court, the Court of Appeals, the High Court, the Industrial Court, and the Environment and Land Court. The subordinate courts consist of the Magistrate's Courts, Courts Martial, and Kadhi Court. Kenya has made significant progress in gender inclusion in its judiciary. In May 2021, Lady Justice Martha Koome became the first female Chief Justice of Kenya. Even though comprehensive judicial reforms have been implemented across the last few decades, segments of the system continue to exhibit corruption. These segments of corruption primarily reside with the lower-level courts, and they threaten the delivery of justice and compromise judicial professionalism.

4.3.4 The County Government

The county governments consist of the county assembly and executive (Kenya Law, 2021b). The executive is headed by a governor directly elected by the citizens and, after that, becomes the highest elected official in the county. The county assembly consists of members of the county assembly as citizens' representatives. The primary objective of decentralization was to devolve power, resources and representation.

Decentralization enables counties to identify priorities, make policies, mobilize resources, budget finances, develop plans; and monitor, evaluate and facilitate citizen decision-making (Kenya Law, 2021b). The wide powers bestowed upon the counties enable the county governments to develop policies that may enhance investments in their areas of jurisdiction. Amendments to the 2010 constitution have produced institutional and legal reforms that have enabled road construction and healthcare facilities.

4.3.5 Separation of Powers

The constitution stipulates that the three branches of government (e.g. legislative, executive and judicial) must be separate and act independently to promote liberty (National Conference of State Legislatures, 2021). The term 'separation of power' refers to the division of government responsibilities into distinct branches to limit any one branch from exercising the core functions of another. The intent is to prevent the concentration of power and provide checks and balances.

4.3.5.1 Challenges to Kenya's Democracy

President Mwai Kibaki's and President Uhuru Kenyatta's governments are widely lauded for political stability and progress compared to past regimes. Both administrations have demonstrated an ability to set cogent strategic economic targets. A major example of this effort relates to Vision 2030, unveiled in 2008. This project seeks to convert Kenya from its present economic structure into a middle-income country by 2030 (Kenya Vision 2030, 2021). This is a goal the country has almost achieved after rebasing the economy. While focusing on the economic, social and political pillars, together with such enablers as the infrastructure, the government intends to pursue a wide range of projects with varying links to a broad range of Kenya's demographic and ethnic sectors. While these goals are ambitious and appropriate at this time in Kenya's history, the success in achieving them is strongly dependent on political stability.

As with any complicated political system, various factors chip away at the desired consistent political stability. In Kenya, strong personal and ethno-regional interests characterized by political coalitions and manipulation often dominate the political scene. Often, the result is a political system based on patronage rather than clear ideological principles. These machinations create intense political polarization in the country, providing a fertile ground for corruption and bribery. Furthermore, political parties follow and reflect the ethno-regional alliances built by political leaders characterized by a high degree of polarization and volatility. However, Kenya has maintained a stronger and more stable democracy in the region.

4.3.5.2 Digital Democracy

Democracy allows all people to participate in meaningful discourse in the decisions that affect the entire society. Digital democracy was developed to expand participation and enhance democracy. Clearly, the many people who use digital platforms daily express their views and protest policies and political decisions, which testifies to the power of electronic arenas of public dialogue. Implicit in a digital democracy is the notion that technology is neutral. This notion is not accurate because of the inequalities and biases that are embedded in digital platforms and access. As more governments and corporations use the Internet and electronic platforms, the more influential social media has limited its inclusiveness. The entrance of money and advertising has allowed anyone wishing to influence an election or voting to free do so without any constraints (Nyabola, 2020).

4.3.5.3 Security, Corporate Governance and Corruption

Whereas the government has continued to pursue reforms geared toward improving the country's security and creating a conducive business environment to attract investments, notable challenges persist. The COVID-19 pandemic has posed health and economic challenges worldwide, and Kenya is no exception. The Kenyan government continues to administer vaccines, encourage the use of masks, and social distancing, control the movement of people, scale-up capacity in health facilities and provide health education (the Republic of Kenya, 2021).

Security and criminality are fairly common in major urban centers. The increase in crime is exacerbated by the fact that security threats are dynamic, unpredictable and constantly evolving. To enhance security, law and order, the government is intended to improve the capacity of the security forces by increasing funding and providing modern and efficient equipment and information systems. In the past, Kenya has suffered acts of terrorism, undermining economic growth and development. Most of these attacks are often unleashed by the Al-Shabaab militia targeting Kenyan security forces and business interests in Wajir, Garissa, Lamu, Nairobi, and Mandera counties. Several reforms have been implemented to counter-terrorism, including enhanced capacity, inter-agency cooperation, international cooperation, and local community involvement (the Republic of Kenya, 2021). Public corruption has been noted as a major concern in Kenya. The response has been implementing various measures that strengthen public finance management. Specifically, reforms undertaken include improving the public procurement system. Moreover, the government has progressively increased allocations to such institutions as the Office of the Director of Public Prosecutions, the Office of the Auditor General, the Ethics and Anti-Corruption Commission, the Assets Recovery Agency, the Criminal Investigations Services, and the Financial Reporting Centre.

Poor corporate governance in public enterprises has been prevalent. To ramp up good corporate governance in state corporations, the government developed a policy for evaluating and training state corporation boards (the Republic of Kenya, 2021).

4.4 Political Risk

Learning about a country's environment is the first step in understanding its business potential. A country risk assessment focuses on both the political and economic conditions in the country. Various questions need to be answered. A country's risk can be comprised of an unstable government, wars, coups, and other political turmoil that can impede or threaten business conduct (Geringer et al., 2020). Political risk is a multidimensional concept that includes economic, sociocultural and political factors (Ellstrand et al., 2002). Whereas internationalization represents a critical strategic decision for any business seeking new markets, low costs, and increased revenues, venturing into new international business arenas can expose a company to various threats. As such, measuring political risk is critical.

The current circumstances portend political risks for commercial investment in Kenya. However, this does not impede investments from occurring. No matter where commercial entities choose to locate, there will always be different investment terrains to maneuver. Kenya's environment presents a relatively stable business environment. Some political factors impact business opportunities both negatively and positively. Investors may shy away from political situations they view perilous to their business ventures. On the other hand, others may view the same circumstances as a boon. For example, lazy institutional and legal frameworks may attract some investors to take advantage of the inherent weaknesses which allow the avoidance of stringent regulations, especially as it relates to labor and tax laws.

The geopolitical risk landscape is more tumultuous and diverse than in the past. The most common political risk-related loss is exchange transfer, political violence, and import/export embargos. Potential tensions include trade wars; South China Sea territorial conflict; the Middle East wars and civil strife mainly in Israel, Palestine, Iran and Syria; coups in Afghanistan, Africa, and Latin America; rising protest movements and civil disorder in several countries; terrorism; cyber security threats; and a significant rise in migrations of political refugees (Marsh, 2021). A volatile geopolitical environment can threaten global businesses' operations, assets, and people.

Studying political risk is an important function of business investors. Knowing what the risk issues are in making country market entry decisions is critical for any business venture. Part of the market research process means studying risk reports. Foreign Direct Investments (FDI) in Kenya has encountered some political risks that have occasionally caused delays and fears for businesses to invest in the country. For example, Kenya has experienced violence after every national election since 1992. Political risks such as terrorism, ethnic tensions, corruption, institutional weaknesses, democratic accountability, and socio-economic circumstances are real. They must be investigated, assessed, and mitigated to ensure positive and productive investments. Ethnic-based political divisions, interference in key institutions, corruption, and impunity have challenged Kenya's democracy.

To resolve these challenges, a new constitution was implemented in 2010 to enhance democracy, accountability, equity and inclusivity. As noted in Chapter 5, this new governance structure has created the process of devolution of government and local control. It appears that the new legal dispensation has achieved some political stability, as exemplified by the 2013 and 2017 elections, which were more peaceful (U.S. Department of State, 2021).

To be safe, all investors need to thoroughly and periodically review Kenya's political risk profile. Keeping informed as to Kenya's political stability and it's short- and long-term prognoses is an important business analytical function that has to be completed often. The democratic stability theory best explains the causes of these risks (Mlilo, 2019). To mitigate political risk, investors may purchase political risk insurance (Malliaropoulou & Duggal, 2021). The covers are available both in the private market as well as the public market. The private market is comprised of such providers as the London-based Lloyd, AIG, XL Catlin, Euler Hermes, Starr Insurance, and Atradius. The public market is characterized by state-backed investment guarantee firms motivated by the government's foreign policy and international development goals. These include national export credit agencies such as the US's Overseas Private Investment Corporation and multilateral organizations such as the World Bank's Multilateral Investment Guarantee Agency, the Asian Development Bank, and the African Trade Insurance Agency. State-backed entities and national and multilateral political risk insurance providers can offer longer, larger and riskier insurance policies compared with the private market.

Political risk insurance is typically purchased by multinational corporations, importers and exporters, project lenders, financial institutions and capital markets, foreign investors, and contractors in industries like construction and engineering.

4.5 International Treaties

4.5.1 Treaties

International trade agreements are critical to a country's overall development. Free trade agreements contribute to greater economic activity and job creation. They promote regional integration with expanded investment in various business sectors, such as intellectual property and e-commerce. Being connected to other parts of the world commercially is part of economic development and a path to a better standard of living. Kenya is a member of many international trade agreements. All of them have been specifically selected to assist various parts of the Kenyan economy and to provide economic development to those who are in need or who are willing to benefit commercially. Below is a list and explanation of the major trade agreements to which Kenya belongs.

4.5.1.1 African Growth Opportunity Act (AGOA)

AGOA is a trade program to establish stronger commercial ties between the United States and sub-Saharan Africa (SSA). The act establishes a preferential trade agreement between the United States and selected countries in the sub-Saharan region. The AGOA was enacted by Congress in May 2000 and renewed in 2025. The legislation significantly enhances market access to the United States for qualifying SSA countries. The law provides for local textile fabric sourcing where it was considered that sufficient quantities were available in AGOA-eligible countries. However, third-country sources are allowed if the denim garments are unavailable locally or regionally (African Growth Opportunity, 2021).

4.5.1.2 African Union (AU)

AU was established in July 2001 to achieve greater unity among the African States. Currently, it has a membership of 55 states. In 2020, AU established the African Continental Free Trade Area agreement, which seeks to create the largest free trade area in the world with a potential market size of 1.3 billion people (African Union, 2021).

4.5.1.3 Bretton Woods Institutions

Bretton Woods Institutions include the International Monetary Fund (IMF), the International Finance Corporation (IFC), the Multilateral Investment Guarantee Agency (MIGA), and the World Bank (World Bank, 2021). IMF provides temporary financial assistance to member countries to help ease balance of payments adjustment as well-economic technical assistance. IFC assists member countries in promoting indigenous enterprises and improving the investment climate through building investment. MIGA formulates an integrated approach to private sector development, including insurance coverage. The World Bank engages in providing credit to member countries for the structural and financial sector, social policy reform, public sector resource management, poverty reduction, and governance improvements, as well as resource mobilization for the physical and social infrastructure. Kenya has been a member of the Bretton Woods Institutions since 1964.

4.5.1.4 Common Market for Eastern and Southern Africa (COMESA)

COMESA Treaty comprises 19 member states, including Kenya. The treaty seeks to recognize, promote and protect human rights; enhance commitment to principles of liberty and the rule of law; and maintain peace and stability in the region. Over time, COMESA has reoriented its focus to forming a large economic and trading unit capable of overcoming trade and investment barriers among the member countries. Furthermore, COMESA has forged trade and investment partnerships with other countries, including the United States (COMESA, 2021).

4.5.1.5 East African Community (EAC)

EAC was created to establish an economic union among the member countries. Currently, the EAC is made up of six-member states, namely Burundi, Kenya, Rwanda, South Sudan, Tanzania and Uganda (East Africa Community, 2021).

EAC has established a customs union and free trade protocols for the member states, which investors can leverage to expand their markets.

4.5.1.6 Intergovernmental Authority on Development (IGAD)

IGAD was formed in January 1986 as an intergovernmental authority on drought and development, and it was revitalized in 1996 as an intergovernmental agency on development in the horn of Africa (IGAD, 2021). Key objectives include promoting joint development strategies and gradually harmonizing macro-economic policies and programs; harmonizing policies about trade, customs, transport, communications, agriculture, and natural resources; promoting free movement of goods, services and people within the region; and creating an enabling environment for foreign, cross-border and domestic trade and investment. Kenya is one of the six-member states of IGAD.

4.5.1.7 Organization of African, Caribbean, and Pacific States (OACPS)

OACPS is composed of 79 states, which are parties to the ACP EC Partnership Agreement, which binds them to the European Union for, among other things, pursuing sustainable development of its members and their gradual integration into the global economy. EU trade with ACP countries has increased over time, particularly in agricultural products (European Commission, 2022). As the primary destination for agricultural and transformed goods from the region, the EU is ACP countries' main trade partner in terms of exports and imports. Key exports include cocoa, coffee and tea, tropical fruits, and spices. The predominant categories of exports are final products, such as cereals, spirits and liqueurs, and dairy products, among others.

4.5.1.8 United Nations (UN)

The UN is an international organization founded in 1945 with a total membership of 193 states. Kenya was admitted into the UN in 1963 and is currently a security Council member (United Nations, 2021). In January 2021, Kenya started its two-year term on the United Nations Security Council, a position that elevates the country's geopolitical position internationally.

4.5.1.9 World Trade Organization (WTO)

WTO provides a forum to resolve trade conflicts between members and to carry on negotiations to further lower and or eliminate tariffs and other trade barriers. It comprises 183 countries, with Kenya joining in 1995 (World Tarde Organization, 2021). WTO provides a good forum for settling commercial disputes for investors.

These treaties and organizations is important to Kenya's business environment and stability. The connections and relationships with these treaties provide an ongoing stable source of business investment that spreads throughout the country. The benefits that accrue from these treaties positively impact the economic growth and development of Kenya.

4.6 Business Obstacles in Kenya

While the Kenyan business environment continues to improve, challenges remain. The top five challenges are corruption, intellectual property rights security; enforcement; unemployment and poverty; and land reforms. Resolution to these problems/challenges requires a concerted effort among both the electorate and the elected policymakers (Kenya-Country Commercial Guide, 2020). None of these challenges are easy to eliminate or mitigate. However, some containment level is necessary for Kenya to become more competitive. Concerted efforts at the national and local governments are necessary to overcome these obstacles. Furthermore, as Kenya develops and aspires to attract more investments, it is critical to strengthen key institutions and enhance governance. Without such remedies, Kenya's business environment will continue to pose serious questions to potential investors.

4.7 Discussion

Since Kenya is a market-oriented economy, it has a good relationship with the Western world and many other countries whose economic foundations are based on capitalism and free markets. Presently, Kenya is considered the financial, commercial, and logistics hub for East Africa. Over the last few decades, Kenya has successfully attracted many Western companies as exporters and investors. Kenya has recognized that the market-oriented approach to economic development has many widespread benefits related to people's standard of living. Kenya's economic success is derived from its people. They are multicultural and multifaceted, which allows them to be versatile in economic, social, and technical activities that are needed in business development. Continued political stability has become a major factor in promoting and enhancing Kenya's economic and social success. The revised constitution devolved government and resulted in the devolved provision of government services. A devolved government empowered citizens and enabled county governments to select development projects that were impactful and meaningful for their respective regions.

4.8 Conclusion

Leaders and politicians have the upper hand in determining the country's direction. Hassan (2020) states that there is a relationship among three major country players, namely the leaders, bureaucrats and residents. How these three actors interact will have a major impact on the country's direction and the quality of life for Kenyans. The interface of these actors' decisions is critical to the country's operation and overall direction. Three arrangements exist among these three actors. Residents can align with the leader through voting and, thus, affect the decisions that the leader's government will ultimately propose. The bureaucrats' loyalty toward the leader determines the operationalization of the leader's visions. Finally, the embeddedness of the bureaucrats among residents affects the bureaucrats' ability to implement the leaders' decisions. As such, the political environment, and the political parties that ultimately win an election, make the policy decisions that affect the country. Politics is always a moving activity. Many factors affect the political dynamics of a country. Kenya is one of those countries that rely upon tradition as a means of electing its leaders. In some ways, the traditional ways are good, but in other ways, they seem to stymie the country by not modernizing the way political processes and affiliations are developed. For decades, inclusiveness politics has been the way of Kenyan politics. The exploitation of tribalism by politicians and the Kenyan influence has been the norm. Predatory and tribal politics diminish the opposition parties. This method of doing politics is not helpful to the country's overall economic development (Shilaho, 2018).

While this approach seems to benefit various sectors of the population, there is a belief that it is not good for the country's overall growth and economic development. Civic citizenship versus ethnic tribalism seems like a better path for modernization. This approach is manifested in the new 2010 constitution, which required the government's devolution. For Kenya's investment environment to remain attractive, there must be a continued commitment by government leaders to create a positive investment and political climate. Kenya has great positive economic and political potential. Its leaders must focus on modernization and future orientation that will move the country toward policies that will provide widespread economic and social benefits for all Kenyans.

References

African Growth Opportunity Act (2021). *About AGOA.* https://agoa.info/about-agoa.html, accessed July 9, 2021.

African Union (2021). *About AU*. http://www.au.int/, accessed July 9, 2021.

Common Market for Eastern and Southern Africa (2021). *COMESA Objectives and Priorities*, https://www.comesa.int/what-is-comesa/

East African Community (2021). *About EAC*, http://www.eac.int/, accessed July 9, 2021.

Ellstrand, A.E., Laszo, T., and Jonathan, L.J. (2002). Board Structure and International Political Risk, *Academy of Management*, 45(4), 769–777.

European Commission (2022). *International Partnerships*, https://international-partnerships. ec.europa.eu/policies/european-development-policy/acp-eu-partnership_en

Geringer, M.J., McNett, J.M., and Ball, D.A. (2020). *International Business*, 2nd edition, New York:McGraw Hill.

Hassan, M. (2020). *Regime Threats and State Solutions*, Cambridge Press.

Inter-Governmental Authority on Development (2021). *About Us*. http://Igad.int/, accessed July 9, 2021.

Kanyingi, K. (2014) Kenya, Democracy and Political Participation. *A review by AfriMAP, Open Society Initiative doe Eastern Africa and the Institute for Development Studies, University of Nairobi*, Open Society Foundation. March 2014.

Kenya-Country Commercial Guide (2020). https://www.trade.gov/knowledge-product/kenya-market-challenges, accessed on July 9, 2021.

Kenya Law (2021a). *The Constitution of Kenya, 2010*. Kenya Law. http://kenyalaw.org/

Kenya Law (2021b). *County Governments Act*. http://kenyalaw.org:8181/exist/

Kenya Vision 2030 (2021). *About Vision 2030*. https://vision2030.go.ke/

Malliaropoulou, A., and Duggal, K. (2021). Political Risk Insurance. Jus Mundi. https://jusmundi.com/en/document/wiki/en-political-risk-insurance

Marsh (2021). *Political Risk Map 2020: Trade Tensions Threaten Political Stability*. https://www.marsh.com/us/services/political-risk/

Mlilo, W.K. (2019). The causes of Kenya's consistently problematic political risk profile, Thesis for Master's Degree Urban-Econ Development Economists. https://www.researchgate.net/publication/335137338_The_causes_of_Kenya's_consistently_problematic_political_risk_profile, accessed July 9, 2021.

National Conference of State Legislatures (2021). Separation of Powers – An Overview, https://www.ncsl.org/research/about-state-legislatures/separation-of-powers-an-overview.aspx

Nyabola, N. (2020). *Digital Democracy, Analogue Politicians: How the Internet Era is Transforming Politic in Kenya*, London: Zed Books.

Republic of Kenya (2021). 2021 Budget Policy Statement. *The National Treasury and Planning*, https://www.treasury.go.ke/budget-policy-statement/

Shilaho, W.K. (2018). *Conclusion: Political Power and Tribalism in Kenya*, 165–175, Palgrave-Macmillan.

United Nations (2021). *United Nations Charter*, https://www.un.org/en/about-us/un-charter

U.S. Department of State (2021). *2021 Investment Climate Statements: Kenya*, https://www.state.gov/reports/2021-investment-climate-statements/kenya/

World Bank (2021). *Member Countries*, https://www.worldbank.org/en/about/leadership/members

World Population Review (2022). *Oil Reserves by Country 2022*, https://worldpopulationreview.com/country-rankings/oil-reserves-by-country

World Trade Organization (2021). *About WTO and Members*, http://www.wto.org//, accessed July 9, 2021.

5 The Economic Climate

5.1 Background

Business is a critical contributor to the economic development of societies. According to Sultan and Haque (2011) and Simuţ and Meşter (2014), some trade determinants have a direct influence on economic growth, while Tekin (2012) determined that exports increase with growth. In Kenya, business is a major source of and catalyst for creating wealth and employment opportunities, markets for goods and services, national income, and infrastructure development (Republic of Kenya, 2020a). Furthermore, the business contributes to reducing poverty, providing government revenue through taxation, supplementing government development efforts through voluntary initiatives, supplying goods and services and complementing general economic development.

5.1.1 Economic Conditions Necessary for Business Development

The key factors that impact business activity include the country's political, legal, economic, technological and social environment; factors of production; access to markets; skilled labor; innovativeness; and infrastructure services (Ismail, A.A., et al., 2020). The economic environment includes economic growth, exchange rates, inflation rates, interest rates, disposable income of consumers and unemployment rates (Fahey & Narayanan, 1986). These factors have direct or indirect long-term effects on business activity and investments in general since they affect the purchasing power of consumers and could change demand/supply models in the economy, as well as in business. Because they are dynamic, organizations have no control over them.

The economy occupies a high-ranking position in every country's priorities. Government policies will normally promote economic growth, including business development. For this reason, governments often go to great lengths to woo investors – both local and foreign – by promulgating policies that create advantageous investments and a conducive business climate. According to the World Bank (2020a), facilitative and enabling

DOI: 10.4324/9781003095156-5

policies are necessary to inspire business activity in the following areas: (i) government approvals and access to physical infrastructure like electricity; (ii) accessing financing; (iii) sanctity of property rights; and (iv) efficient resolution of disputes. Moreover, the Organization for Economic Co-operation and Development (OECD) contends that attractive conditions for business investment are created by formulating reforms in such critical areas as (a) investment policy and investment promotion; (b) trade and competition policy; (c) fiscal policy; (d) corporate and public governance; (e) ethical business practices; (f) human resource development; (g) infrastructure and financial sector development; and (h) public governance (2014).

Empirical evidence shows a strong relationship between economic growth and foreign direct investment and trade (i.e. exports, imports openness, trade restrictions) (Boldeanu and Constantinescu, 2015). Furthermore, Simuț and Meșter (2014) identified a positive correlation and causality between exports, openness, and economic growth. Studies also support that countries with better institutions, coupled with other growth drivers, develop faster (Acemolu et al., 2005). Economic institutions, through investments in physical and human capital and technology, as well as production organization, bear a significant influence on the incentives of major economic actors in society.

In addition, governance is considered an important determinant of economic growth and investment, and business activity. According to Rodrick (2000) the following five types of institutional governance frameworks impact economic growth: property rights, regulatory institutions, institutions for macroeconomic stabilization, institutions for social insurance and institutions of conflict management. Arusha (2009) demonstrated that countries with high governance grow faster than those with weak governance regimes. Murphy et al. (1993) and Mauro (1995) contended that corruption harms growth by affecting innovation and other start-up activities, which may reduce productivity.

Enhanced public expenditure is a strategy often used to stimulate economic growth, especially during periods of recession. Ghosh and Gregoriou (2008) found that public spending significantly and positively affected growth. Meanwhile, Benos (2009) affirmed that infrastructure and human capital significantly affected long-term growth. However, to avoid the otherwise unintended consequences of bloated public spending, such as over-taxation, and inflation, caution needs to be exercised.

Unsurprisingly, investors and business managers invest significant resources to learn about the external business environment that affects businesses. Knowledge of economic conditions, a major part of this environment, is vital because it informs which types of investments and business decisions to make and which strategies to adopt to succeed.

5.2 Kenya's Economic System

5.2.1 General Overview

An economic system is a means by which societies or governments organize and distribute available resources, services, and goods across a geographic region or country (Ericson, 2013). Furthermore, it regulates the factors of production, including land, capital, and labor. Economists also use the terms command and market economies, or a mix of the two, to describe an economic system.

In a market economy, also called an open economy, economic decisions are determined by the forces of supply and demand (Jessop 2002). A market economy describes an economy where consumers and producers voluntarily interact and exchange without legal compulsion (Ericson, 2013). The quantities traded and the price at which trade occurs is determined exclusively by suppliers and consumers. Typically, market economies allow for the direct interaction of consumers and producers pursuing their self-interest. Contrary to the notion that such markets operate without legal regulation, the participants must conform to laws concerning health and safety, weights and measures, labeling requirements, and so on. However, the essential point of these rules is that they lay down the basis for property rights and contract law without unduly interrupting the forces of supply and demand.

Attributed to Otto Neurath, the concept of a command or planned economy refers to an environment in which economic effort is devoted to goals passed down from a ruler or central authority (Ericson, 2013). Governments own and allocate the factors of production, such as land, capital, and resources. This method of economic management is referred to as central planning, and economies that exclusively use central planning are called command economies. In other words, governments direct or command resources to be used in particular ways.

In the real world, most economies are mixed; they combine elements of command and market systems (Ericson, 2013). Many countries in Africa, including Kenya, as well as those in Asia, Europe, and North America, are at different positions of the mixed economy spectrum. On the other hand, countries such as Cuba and North Korea have policies that tend toward a command economy.

Kenya has a market-based economy, similar to Western capitalist economies, with a liberalized external trade system and a few state enterprises (Mwega and Ndung'u, 2008). The government influences economic decisions indirectly (through policies), as well as through direct participation in economic activities. Key sectors of the economy, including agriculture, manufacturing, tourism, communication, banking, and financing, are largely liberalized. Since 1993, the exchange rate has been uncontrolled, and imports and foreign exchange transactions have been deregulated (Ndung'u, 1997), with limited control by the Central Bank of Kenya, the country's monetary authority. Since Kenya's independence, this structure has been generally favorable to domestic and foreign investment, creating a robust and steadily growing private sector.

As discussed in Chapter 3 and elsewhere, indirect government influence is exercised by regulating the economy through fiscal and monetary policies. There are laws governing health, consumer protection, property rights, and contract enforcement. In the same vein, the government has created conditions that are conducive to investments. On the other hand, direct influence is represented by the state acting as a consumer and producer of goods and services. The public sector is a major consumer of goods and services, including fuel, electricity, water, stationery, machinery, houses, etc. The government also plays the role of a producer. For example, the government of Kenya is a producer of agricultural goods and services, transport services, electricity, and other consumer goods, mainly through partnerships with private sector investors.

5.2.2 Investment Climate Reforms

Kenya has enacted several regulatory reforms to simplify and facilitate foreign and local investment, including creating an export processing zone (USA State Department, 2020) and tax incentives for investment in certain sectors, as noted in Chapter 3. According to the World Bank's Ease of Doing Business (World Bank, 2020a), significant improvements have been made in Kenya's investment climate in the following notable areas: business approval processes through institutional reforms and digitization of government services; access to credit; business regulations through the revising and realigning of over 50 business-related statutes; physical infrastructure by improving access to water and electricity; and land and business registries via improving capacity.

Compared to the Sub-Sharan African region's average annual inflation of 7.9 percent, Kenya's inflation index rose to 5.3 percent in 2021, which is attributable mainly to increased food prices, global oil price increases, the COVID-19 pandemic and costs of energy (Kenya National Bureau of Statistics, 2021). In December 2020, the unemployment rate in Kenya stood at almost 12.86 percent and is projected to trend around 12.30 percent in 2021 (International Monetary Fund, 2021). In 2019, Kenya's labor force was 22.3 million people, 88.3 percent of whom were employed, while 11.7 percent were unemployed (Kenya National Bureau of Statistics, 2020). Of the 13.7 million young adults aged 18 and 34, 61 percent were working, while 39 percent were unemployed. Even though Kenya provides an abundant youthful, well-skilled labor force, the young adult unemployment rate stood at 7.3 percent in 2020 and continues to be a major challenge.

5.2.3 Key Economic Sectors

Agriculture remains the backbone of the Kenyan economy, contributing one-third of the GDP (Kenya National Bureau of Statistics, 2020). About

75 percent of Kenya's population of roughly 48.5 million work at least part-time in the agricultural sector, including livestock and pastoral activities. Kenya exports coffee, tea, flowers and apparels.

Tourism is the second largest contributor of foreign exchange, after agriculture, due to the country's abundant fauna and flora (Kenya National Bureau of Statistics, 2020); however, the COVID-19 pandemic has caused the number of visitors to drop, dealing with the sector a major setback.

The services sector, representing about 55 percent of Kenya's GDP, is a major economic driver (Kenya National Bureau of Statistics, 2020). As the sub-Saharan African distribution center, telecommunications hub, and financial axis, Kenya is the region's leading producer and exporter of services. Furthermore, Kenya has a wide range of well-developed service industries, with robust service providers in distribution and transportation, financial services, information and communications, business and professional services, and education services. Other key industries are forestry, fishing, mining, manufacturing, and energy.

Kenya's main exports are horticulture, tea, apparel and clothing accessories, coffee, and iron and steel, contributing 59 percent of exports (Kenya National Bureau of Statistics, 2020). Thirty-eight percent of Kenya's total exports are destined for within Africa, making Africa the leading market for the country's exports, followed by Europe. The East African Community (EAC) market accounts for 62.6 percent of Kenya's African export market. Major imports are petroleum, industrial pieces of machinery, iron, and steel, motor vehicles, plastics, and pharmaceutical products, representing about 49.5 percent of the total import value. China, India, United Arab Emirates, Japan and Saudi Arabia are the key sources of Kenya's imports.

5.2.4 Digital Economy

The digital economy is pivotal in expanding Kenya's economic development. The information and communications technology (ICT) sector trended about 11 percent annual growth since 2016, significantly contributing to the county's economic development (World Bank, 2020b). Kenya has rapidly embraced mobile communications technologies, becoming a world leader in the adoption of digital payments, with the current number of mobile money accounts surpassing the total population by about 12 percent. (World Bank, 2021b). Kenya has also increasingly become a center of innovation, propelled mainly by a large reservoir of talented and well-educated young people, as well as government investments in ICT infrastructure. The government has scaled internet infrastructure development investments, increasing internet use and bolstering the uptake of e-commerce and digital services. Entrepreneurship, innovation and a supportive business environment have catalyzed several digitally-enabled startups and investments by major multinational tech companies, labelling Kenya as the 'Silicon Savannah' and helping to fuel services-led growth.

5.2.5 *Kenya's Vision 2030*

Kenya's economic development agenda is outlined in Vision 2030, a blueprint articulating the country's developmental aspirations and aiming to create a prosperous, globally competitive nation with a high quality of life by 2030 (Kenya Vision 2030, 2020). In 2017, President Uhuru Kenyatta announced the 'Big Four Agenda' development priority areas of manufacturing, universal healthcare, affordable housing, and food security under the Vision 2030 Third Medium Plan (the Republic of Kenya, 2020b) as a means of realizing faster economic development. Kenya's Cabinet Administrative Secretary for Foreign Affairs has stated that these four pillars present many investment opportunities: 'Kenya is on a very positive trajectory with all fundamentals just perfect for a robust and bullish business environment that has been injected with the impetus of the Big 4 Agenda championed by President Uhuru Kenyatta himself, focusing on Manufacturing, Affordable Housing, Universal Health and Food Security.'[1]

5.3 Monetary and Fiscal Systems and Policies

Typically, economies are managed through two main tools – monetary policy and fiscal policy. Central banks, the major monetary authorities, indirectly target activity by influencing the money supply through adjusting interest rates, bank reserve requirements, and the purchase and sale of government securities and foreign exchange (Central Bank of Kenya, 2021a). Fiscal policies, on the other hand, are applied to influence the economy by changing the level and types of taxes, the extent and composition of spending, and the degree and form of borrowing.

5.3.1 *Monetary System*

This section begins with definitions of the various forms of monetary systems before discussing Kenya's monetary system. A monetary system is a set of frameworks, policies, and institutions by which governments create money in economies and shape payment conditions in foreign trade (Mikita, M., 2015). Relevant institutions may include the mint, the central bank, the treasury, and other financial institutions. There are three common types of monetary systems – commodity money, commodity-based money, and fiat money. Currently, fiat money is the most common type of monetary system in the world.

Commodity money is made up of precious metals or other commodities that have intrinsic value. In other words, the monetary system uses the commodity physically in terms of currency. For example, gold and silver coins have been commonly used throughout history as a form of money. Fiat money, however, is represented by currency, the approved legal tender, i.e., the government guarantees the currency's value. Today, most fiat money is in the form of bank balances and records of credit or debit card purchases.

Money is used as a means of payment or a medium of exchange, therefore eliminating the problem of coincidence of needs associated with a barter system. It is also a standard unit of measurement that can be used to price things and compare values. Money can also be used to store value and thus becomes an asset itself; however, money may not be a good store of value since it loses value over time due to inflation.

The Central Bank of Kenya (CBK) is responsible for Kenya's monetary system (Kenya Law, 2021). It formulates monetary policy and regulates banking financial institutions. It also regulates the money supply, assists in the development of the monetary, credit, and banking system, acts as a banker and financial adviser to the government, and grants short-term or seasonal loans. The CBK's key policy objectives are to achieve sustainable stability in the general level of prices; foster the liquidity, solvency, and proper functioning of a stable market-based financial system; and support the economic policy of the government. Other functions are to formulate and implement foreign exchange policy; to hold and manage foreign exchange reserves; to license and supervise authorized dealers; to formulate and implement policies for promoting efficient and effective payment, clearing, and settlement systems; to act as banker, adviser and fiscal agent to the government; and to issue currency notes and coins.

The CBK determines the base or lowest rate of interest it charges on loans to banks, also known as the Central Bank Rate (CBR), which signals its stance on monetary policy (Central Bank of Kenya, 2021b). Low CBR suggests a desire to release liquidity, while high CBR is used to mop up excess liquidity and stem inflation. Lending rates are determined by market-driven credit pricing.

Kenya's exchange rate regime is liberalized, with no restrictions on the repatriation of profits by foreign firms (USA Department of Trade, 2021). Between independence and 1974, the exchange rate was pegged to the U.S. Dollar, and until 1982, the rate was determined through a crawling peg in real terms. Since 1993, the exchange has been liberalized – it floats freely according to the forces of demand and supply. The CBK rarely and cautiously intervenes in the foreign exchange market to curb volatility, bolster the required stock of foreign reserves, and make government payments and inject or withdraw liquidity in the market.

Kenya's monetary unit is the Kenyan Shilling (KES) (CBK, 2020a). The exchange rate for the KES against major world currencies has depreciated due to the global recession experienced in 2020 and 2021. In November 2020, the exchange rates were as follows: 110.07 KES to the U.S. dollar, 150.11 KES to the Sterling Pound, and 133.73 KES to the Euro.

5.3.2 Fiscal Policy

Government spending, taxation, and borrowing are the three major fiscal policy instruments influencing the economy. Simply put, fiscal policy uses government spending and taxation to manage the economy. Fiscal policy is used to promote strong and sustainable growth and reduce poverty. Furthermore, fiscal policy significantly impacts business activity – for instance, a favorable tax regime is more likely to attract investments and vice versa. As noted in section 5.2, government spending and borrowing also impact business activity.

Before 1930, the prevalent approach to economic management was limited government interference, also known as a laissez-faire approach. Following the stock market crash of 1929 and the subsequent Great Depression, policymakers advocated for governments to play a more proactive role in the economy. After that, countries reduced government involvement – with the forces of demand and supply left to determine the allocation of goods and services. When the global financial crisis of 2008 threatened worldwide recession, however, many countries returned to a more active fiscal policy, compelling governments to support financial systems, jump-start.

Responding to the COVID-19 pandemic, Kenya has implemented an economic recovery strategy, the focus of which is to accelerate growth in private sector investment; enhance allocations to strengthen healthcare systems; support recovery and growth of micro, small and medium enterprises; and implement economic stimulus programs. Other responses and mitigation strategies include addressing economic governance more aggressively; enhancing investment in information technology and digital infrastructure; facilitating clean, green, and resilient growth; bolstering the economy's resilience to global shocks; better disaster preparedness; and international cooperation (the Republic of Kenya, 2021).

Fiscal policy that increases aggregate demand directly through an increase in government spending is typically called expansionary or 'loose.' By contrast, fiscal policy is often considered contractionary or 'tight,' if it reduces demand via lower spending. As discussed in Chapter 3, government spending in Kenya continues to increase over time as it leans more toward the non-productive sector. Public debt, currently estimated at 71.47 percent of GDP (Statista, 2021), has also increased significantly with the risk of raising the debt distress level. The government's eagerness to borrow internally may crowd out the private sector in the domestic credit market, leading to reduced investment activities. Overall, the positive effects of increased government expenditure and borrowing must be weighed against the negative ones.

The government also uses taxation as a tool to promote investments. As discussed in Chapter 3, Kenya provides investment incentives through tax holidays in the hospitality, manufacturing, housing, and film industries. Tax incentives are also available to enterprises operating in the over 40 designated export processing zones in Athi River, Embu, Kerio Valley, Kilifi, Mombasa, Muranga and Nairobi (Export Processing Zones Authority, 2021a). Key incentives in the zones include perpetual exemption from paying stamp duty, value-added tax, and customs import duty; 100 percent investment deduction on new investments; and a ten-year withholding and corporate tax holiday (Export Processing Zones Authority, 2021b).

Under Vision 2030, Kenya has also established special economic zones (SEZs), located at Dongo Kundu and Free Port, in Mombasa, Lamu, Kisumu, and Naivasha, respectively (Special Economic Zones Authority, 2021). The fiscal incentives associated with these SEZs include 10 percent corporate tax for the first ten years and 15 percent for subsequent years; customs import duty and value-added tax exemptions; 100 percent investment allowance on buildings and machinery; and exemption from paying stamp duty and withholding tax. Other advantages are the protection of business revenue and assurance of repatriating profits.

Key fiscal policy institutions in Kenya are the National Treasury, the National Assembly, and the Kenya Revenue Authority (KRA). The National Treasury performs the following functions: it formulates, implements, and monitors macro-economic policies involving expenditure and revenue; prepares the national budget, as well as executing and controlling approved budgetary resources; and manages the level and composition of national public debt, national guarantees and other financial obligations of the national government (Kenya Law, 2021). Likewise, the National Assembly determines the allocation of national revenue between the levels of government, appropriates funds for expenditure by the national government and other national state bodies and exercises oversight over national revenue and its expenditure (Kenya Law, 2021). The KRA is responsible for collecting revenue on behalf of the government. It also assesses, collects and accounts for all revenues while advising the government on all matters relating to the administration and collection of revenue (Kenya Revenue Authority 2021).

5.4 Financial Services System

5.4.1 Introduction

According to the OECD, a financial system consists of institutional units and markets that interact, typically in a complex manner, to mobilize funds for investment and provide facilities (including payment systems) to finance commercial activity (OECD, 2020). According to the OECD (2020, p. 1), a financial system can also be described as 'a densely interconnected network of intermediaries, facilitators, and markets that serve three major purposes: allocating capital, sharing risks, and facilitating all types of trade, including intertemporal exchange.'[2]

The system's main function is to efficiently link borrowers to lenders, thereby facilitating a higher level of saving and investment in the economy than would otherwise be the case. Borrowers include investors, entrepreneurs, and other economic agents, such as domestic households, governments, established businesses, and foreigners with potentially profitable business ideas but limited financial resources. In general, borrowers require access to funds of varying amounts to finance debt and capital investment. Lenders or savers include domestic households, businesses, governments, and foreigners with excess funds drawn from customers' deposits, their resources and from borrowing. The financial system also helps to link risk-averse entities (hedgers) to less risk-averse entities (speculators).

Financial systems allow funds to be allocated, invested, or moved between economic sectors. They also enable individuals and companies to share the associated risks. An alternative to bartering, a modern financial system may include banks, financial markets, financial instruments, and financial services. Financial markets provide a forum within which financial claims can be traded under established rules of conduct and can facilitate the management and transformation of risk. Inevitably, policymakers pay, or ought to pay, close attention to managing risks associated with financial systems, which can otherwise wreak havoc on an economy.

Kenya's financial system comprises banking, insurance, capital markets, pensions, SACCO societies, industry, and unregulated financial services providers (Central Bank of Kenya, 2020a). The CBK notes that this system is supported by a robust infrastructure of financial markets that facilitates payments, settlements, and custodial services. Furthermore, it is highly interconnected, diversified, and segmented, with increasing cross-border operations. Invariably, this adds to the complexity of the financial sector, which in turn creates opportunities for non-operating holding companies to manage the operations of these complex entities.

To keep abreast with the rest of the world, the Kenyan financial system has adopted financial, and technological innovations (FinTechs), which have transformed the sector in terms of products and services (Central Bank of Kenya, 2020a). This new development has brought gains in resource use and profit maximization. For instance, besides elevating the country's competitiveness, mobile phone-based financial services have led to growth and employment opportunities as they continue to present opportunities for new investment. These services have also created potential risks, including fraud and cyber security attacks, which industry players and regulators must figure out how to manage.

Over the last ten years, the transformation of financial services in Kenya has been impressive. Recent global data shows that 83 percent of adults have a formal account that allows them to save, send and/or receive money (Harvard Business Review, 2021), making Kenya a leader in sub-Saharan Africa. Indeed, Kenya outperforms both the global average as well as many middle-income countries such as Chile, Brazil, India, Mexico and Russia.

In 2020, Kenya's financial system was reported to be generally stable and capable of withstanding financial shocks associated with the COVID-19 pandemic (Central Bank of Kenya, 2020a). The sector is characterized by robust technology, alternative distribution channels, increased financial inclusion levels and a stable regulatory environment.

5.4.2 Banking Industry in Kenya

A banking system is a group or network of institutions and laws that provide various financial services (Central Bank of Kenya, 2020b). These institutions are responsible for operating a payment system, offering credit, managing deposits and providing investment services. Banking systems are part of the wider financial services system, and they bear a major influence on the functioning of the 'money economy' of a country. Because deposits occupy a central position in the country's money supply, the banking system is closely regulated by the monetary authorities to ensure stability in the economy.

At its most basic, banking involves an institution holding money on behalf of customers that is payable on demand. The banking system also provides credit for investment and personal needs. Many banks also perform other services for a fee, including bank guarantees and letters of undertaking.

In some countries, banks provide investment and insurance services. Except for Islamic banks, banking almost always involves the payment of interest on deposits and the reception of interest on credit. Investment banking entails trading or dealing with capital markets. Many banks, like most business enterprises, are profit-seekers. They obtain profits by charging the highest possible interest for credit and paying the least possible interest on deposits.

The history of banking in Kenya can be traced to a small banking sector with foreign-owned banks that predominantly served the interests of the foreign and colonial community (Central Bank of Kenya, 2021c). By 1911, there were three banks established in Kenya: (1) the National Bank of India with branches in Mombasa, Nairobi, Nakuru and Kisumu; (2) the Standard Bank of South Africa operating in Mombasa, Nairobi, Nakuru and Kisumu; and (3) Kathiawad and Ahmedabad Banking Corporation in Mombasa. The National Bank of South Africa, which was to become Barclays Bank DCO in 1926, arrived in Mombasa in 1916. Other banks that came onto the scene were ABN-AMRO from the Netherlands in 1951, Habib Bank from Pakistan in 1956, Ottoman Bank from Turkey in 1958, and Commercial Bank of Africa in 1962 (UNCTAD, 2008).

Kenya's first locally owned commercial bank was the Co-operative Bank of Kenya, which was initially a cooperative society started in 1968 to serve the growing farming communities. In the same year, the National Bank of Kenya was also created as the first fully-owned government bank. In 1971, the Kenya Commercial Bank was formed following the merger of the National and Grindlays Banks, with the government owning a 60 percent stake. Between 1990 and 1999 saw, a proliferation of banks, which unfortunately was also characterized by instability and failure.

The current Kenyan banking sector constitutes the Central Bank of Kenya as the regulatory authority, 42 banking institutions, nine representative offices of foreign banks, 14 microfinance banks, three reference bureaus, 19 money remittance providers, eight non-operating bank holding companies and 69 foreign exchange (forex) bureaus (Central Bank of Kenya, 2021c). Twenty-three of the 40 privately owned banks are locally owned, while 17 are foreign-owned. All licensed forex bureaus, microfinance banks, credit reference bureaus, money remittance providers, and nonoperating bank holding companies are privately owned.

Kenya's digital technologies are rapidly growing and providing solutions for credit availability and investment opportunities. Supported by the high mobile access and use, which has surpassed 100 percent active customer subscriptions of 46.6 million, Kenya continues to attract attention to financial technology innovations (CFA Institute Research Foundation, 2020). Moreover, other technologies have recently been introduced to support banking, like blockchain and artificial intelligence, which are seen as effective tools to curb corruption, land fraud, and election disputes, as well as to enhance the level of integrity, security, and reliability for the information it manages.

5.4.3 Insurance Sector

The primary purpose of insurance is to reduce exposure to the effects of particular risks; however, the insurance industry also contributes to economic growth by providing financial security, contributing to financial stability, mobilizing savings, and promoting direct and indirect investments (Insurance Regulatory Authority, 2021a). It also enhances efficiency in resource allocation, reduces transaction costs and disseminates financial services. Insurance companies are a primary part of the financial system, as well as significant tax payers.

The history of the development of commercial insurance in Kenya is closely related to the colonial administration. Initially, British insurers established agency offices to fill the void, later opening branches that were converted into fully-fledged insurance companies. By June 2021, there were 56 registered insurers and five reinsurers in Kenya (Insurance Regulatory Authority, 2021b).

The five reinsurers are Kenya Reinsurance Corporation Limited, East Africa Reinsurance Company Limited, Continental Reinsurance Company Limited, Ghana Reinsurance Company Kenya Limited and Waica Reinsurance Kenya Limited. Two regional reinsurers include PTA Reinsurance Company (ZEP-RE) and Africa Reinsurance Corporation, while the Kenya Reinsurance Corporation is the only local reinsurer. The Africa Trade Insurance Agency provides insurance, coinsurance, and reinsurance, as well as guaranteeing against political, commercial, and noncommercial risks within the continent. Only two foreign reinsurers, CICA-Re and Scor Global P&C SE operate liaison offices in Kenya.

Insurance in Kenya is regulated by the Insurance Regulatory Authority (IRA), a statutory government agency established in 2006 (Insurance Regulatory Authority, 2021a). The IRA regulates, supervises, and develops the insurance industry. Insurance penetration and accessibility have been improving due to the growing middle class, rapid urbanization, devolution of governmental duties, and massive infrastructural development.

5.4.4 Pension Industry

Savings from pension funds are a significant catalyst for enhancing economic growth by securing the future of pensioners, which in turn provides long-term capital for development while deepening that capital (World Bank, 2020c). The current pension systems in Kenya can be traced back to the post-independence era, with the first indigenous pension fund organization, the National Social Security Fund (NSSF), being established in 1965 (Njuguna and Otsola, 2011). Like many other countries, Kenya's pension system comprises several types of funding schemes, namely contributory, defined provident, and pension funds.

The sector comprises four main pillars: the NSSF, Civil Servants Pension Scheme, Occupational Retirement Schemes, and Individual Retirement Schemes. Pension supervision and regulation is performed by the Retirement Benefits Authority (RBA) (Retirement of Benefits Authority, 2021). The NSSF scheme covers people in formal employment, such as traders and self-employed individuals, as well as some workers in the informal sector (Kenya Law, 2020). All employers are required by law to enroll their employees with the NSSF. The employer matches the employee's pension contribution based on the employee's salary. Self-employed persons contribute a set percentage of their monthly income. The public service pension scheme caters to all civil service members on a non-contributory basis.

In 2019, 22 percent of the total labor force had pension coverage, with most of those enrolled drawn from the formal sector (Retirement of Benefits Authority, 2021). The industry has been relatively stable, with an overall risk score of 3.09 in 2019 but below the desired overall risk score of 2.88 (Retirement of Benefits Authority, 2021). The COVID-19 pandemic has exacerbated the pension risk situation. The Retirement Benefits Authority and the government will need to continue monitoring pension funds and institute measures to ensure stability and growth in the industry post-pandemic.

5.4.5 SACCO Societies Industry

A savings and credit cooperative (SACCO) is a cooperative financial organization that is democratically operated by and for its members to accumulate savings and create a source of credit for the members at reasonable interest rates (Kenya Law, 2012a). In some Western countries, SACCOs are referred to as credit unions. Today, Kenya's SACCO societies not only provide credit to their members, but they also offer investment opportunities, support agricultural activity, create employment, and augment housing solutions, among other benefits. Additionally, SACCOs are among Kenya's leading contributors to capital for economic development. In 2019 President Uhuru Kenyatta lauded the critical role cooperatives play in the country's growth while underlining that they account for 45 percent of Kenya's GDP and 30 percent of national savings and deposits (the Republic of Kenya, 2019). In addition to their traditional role of enhancing agricultural and livestock ventures, the government has identified Kenyan SACCOs in its Visions 2030 as potential providers of 25 percent of housing in urban areas.

In the African continent, Kenya is a leader in the SACCO movement, with the sector representing 5.7 percent of the total assets to GDP ratio, followed by Rwanda and Ethiopia, with 3.0 percent and 0.7 percent, respectively (Central Bank of Kenya, 2020a). Recent enhancements of the legal and regulatory environments have spurred growth in and increased access to the SACCO industry, resulting in SACCO participation by 28.4 percent of the adult population as of December 2019. Furthermore, industry growth has been sparked by the rapid adoption of technology, innovations in financial services, new product and the opening of the common membership bond.

5.4.6 Mobile Financial Services

There are more than 20 digital credit services in Kenya, and new services continue to enter the scene (Kenya National Bureau of Statistics, 2020). With Safaricom's flagship M-Pesa (*Pesa* is a Kiswahili word for money) mobile banking innovation, Kenya is the 'fintech' pioneer in both the region and on the African continent. M-Pesa enjoys about 96 percent of the mobile money market share. In contrast, the market balance is distributed among Airtel Money, Telkom Kenya's T-Kash, and Equity Bank's Equitel Money (Communications Authority of Kenya, 2021). M-Pesa dominates this market segment in terms of active subscribers, number of transactions, and value of transactions. The total amount of mobile money transactions in Kenya reached US$52 Billion in 2021, and the total number of mobile money accounts in Kenya reached over 68 Million (Central Bank of Kenya, 2021d).

In Kenya, most adults have an account with a mobile money service provider, which manages their finances through digital technology. This innovation has made banking services available to every person in Kenya for the first time. Remitting money transfers of various amounts from mobile devices provides convenience and flexibility. The unique thing about M-Pesa and other such innovations is that the recipient does not need internet access, only the ability to receive and send text messages. Therefore, even without a smartphone, an individual can enact various financial transactions, from complex banking to riding public transportation (matatu) to securing vegetables from a *Mama Mboga* (female vegetable vendor). The recipients, particularly the rural population, save money when retrieving cash and save the need to travel to urban centers where banks are located to collect their money. Mobile money services are also ideal for making payments, eliminating the need to carry cash and cut cheques.

5.5 Capital Markets

Capital markets or securities markets facilitate capital formation by linking borrowers to savers in the economy. They also intermediate the buying and selling of securities with medium- and long-term maturity, mainly through the stock exchange (CFA Institute of Research Foundation, 2020). Instruments traded in capital markets include equities, derivatives, treasury bills and bonds, corporate bonds, and commercial papers.

Key players in the capital markets are investors, issuers, dealers, brokers, financial intermediaries and regulators. Investors provide their savings to the financial markets for a return on capital. Issuers are domestic or foreign governments, corporations, or other institutions that mobilize funds from investors by issuing securities. Financial intermediaries are commercial banks, dealers, and brokers who act as a link between buyers and sellers by facilitating the movement of funds between capital-deficient parties and parties with excess capital.

Before and in the time immediately after independence, the capital market in Kenya predominately served the needs of the private sector rather than the government, whose main source of capital was foreign aid and grants. Over the years, Kenya's capital market has experienced robust growth, with 65 companies currently listed (Nairobi Securities Exchange, 2021a).

The Capital Markets Authority (CMA) of Kenya was formed through legislation to supervise, license, and monitor the activities of financial market intermediaries and all other players in the capital market to ensure that the markets function properly (Kenya Law, 2012b). Kenya, through CMA, is a member of the International Organization of Securities Commissions, the main international body that sets standards and best practices in securities regulation.

The Nairobi Securities Exchange (NSE) is the only stock exchange in Kenya. The NSE facilitates trade in stocks and shares, among other capital market instruments. The NSE was established in 1954 and was the first stock exchange established to cater to Kenya, Uganda, and Tanzania during the British colonial administration (CFA Institute Research, 2020). In 1977, when the East African Community collapsed, the NSE became a fully Kenyan outfit, with all the non-Kenyan companies delisted and nationalized in their respective countries of Uganda and Tanzania. Besides equities, the stock exchanges provide a debt market for trading government and corporate bonds.

Kenya's official capital market began in 1997 with the first government security issuance. The first company to be listed on a stock exchange was Kenya Commercial Bank in 1988 (Nairobi Securities Exchange, 2021b). Today, Kenya's equity market segments are the main investment market segment, the alternative investment market segment, and the growth enterprise market segment. Furthermore, the NSE hosts debt securities, government, and corporate issues, real estate investment trusts, and an exchange-traded fund based on gold bullion.

5.6 Discussion

Kenya has a strong and stable economy, a strong track record of innovation, a relatively good communication infrastructure, an abundant and young skilled workforce and strong institutions within the region; however, the effects of the recent COVID-19 pandemic, high public debt and a high rate of young adult unemployment may depress the economy and reverse the gains made so far. A lack of judicial effectiveness, poor governance, government integrity, and vulnerabilities associated with fiscal health are the major challenges to the country's investment climate (World Bank, 2021a). Successful policy implementation will likely undermine risks like drought, lack of security, corruption, and political squabbling.

5.7 Conclusion

Favorable economic factors are likely to attract investors to consider Kenya as an ideal and competitive investment location for the East African market and the entire African continent. This is buttressed by the government's continued efforts to implement reforms for creating a conducive investment climate, especially through trade liberalization, investment incentives, creating capacity in the public sector, infrastructure development, and other trade-friendly policies.

Investors considering Kenya as an investment destination will find a strong network of financial services comparable to major the capitals of Western economies. There is a wide variety of banks, insurance services, and investment bankers, as well as a securities market and a host of other financial services that support business development. Kenya's financial sector provides one of the most lucrative investment opportunities in the region.

Notes

1 Republic of Kenya (2021). President Uhuru's Big 4 Agenda to Benefit from US-Kenya business Forum. Ministry of Foreign Affairs. Retrieved from https://www.mfa.go.ke/
2 OECD (2020). Glossary of Statistical Terms. Financial System. Retrieved from https://stats.oecd.org/glossary/detail.asp?ID=6189

References

Acemoglu, D., Johnson, S., and Robinson, A.J. (2005). *Institutions as a Fundamental Cause of Long-Run Growth*. Handbook of Economic Growth, Volume IA. Philippe Aghion and Steven N. Durlauf O 2005 Elsevier B.V. 001: lO.l016/Sl574-W84(05) OloW-3

Arusha, C. (2009). Government Expenditure, Governance, and Economic Growth, *Comparative Economic Studies*, 51, 401–418. 10.1057/ces.2009.7.

Benos, N. (2009). Iscal Policy and Economic Growth: Empirical Evidenc from EU Countries. *Munich Personal RePEc Archive*. Retrieved from https://mpra.ub.uni-muenchen.de/19174/1/MPRA_paper_19174.pdf

Boldeanu, T.F. and Constantinescu, L. (2015). The Main Determinants Affecting Economic Growth, *Bulletin of the Transilvania University of Brașov Series V: Economic Sciences*, 8(57) No. 2–2015.

Central Bank of Kenya (2020a). The Kenya Financial Stability Report. October 2020, Issue No. 11. Retrieved from https://www.centralbank.go.ke/uploads/financial_sector_stability/

Central Bank of Kenya (2020b). Bank Supervision Annual Report 2019. Retrieved from https://www.centralbank.go.ke/reports/bank-supervision-and-banking-sector-reports/

Central Bank of Kenya (2021a). Our Mission. Retrieved from https://www.centralbank.go.ke/

Central Bank of Kenya (2021b). Central Bank Rate. Retrieved from https://www.centralbank.go.ke/rates/central-bank-rate/

Central Bank of Kenya (2021c). Development of Banking in Kenya. Retrieved from https://www.centralbank.go.ke/banking-development

Central Bank of Kenya (2021d). Mobile Payments. Retrieved from https://www.centralbank.go.ke/national-payments-system/mobile-payments

Central Bank of Kenya (2021b). Inflation Rates. Retrieved from https://www.centralbank.go.ke/inflation-rates/

CFA Institute Research Foundation (2020). African Capital Markets: Challenges and Opportunities. Retrieved from https://www.cfainstitute.org/-/media/documents/article/

Communications Authority of Kenya (2021). Statistics. Retrieved from https://www.centralbank.go.ke/national-payments-system/mobile-payments

Ericson, R. (2013). Command Economy and its Legacy in The Oxford Handbook of the Russian Economy. *Edited by Michael Alexeev and Shlomo Weber*. Print Publication Date: Jul 2013 Subject: Economics and Finance, Public Economics and Policy, Economic Development Online Publication Date: Oct 2013. DOI: 10.1093/oxford he/9780199759927.013.0002

Export Processing Zones Authority (2021a). Our Regions. Retrieved from https://epzakenya.com/our-regions/

Export Processing Zones Authority (2021b). EPZ Program. Retrieved from https://epzakenya.com/epz-program/

Fahey, L. and Narayanan, V.K. (1986). *Macroenvironmental Analysis For Strategic Management*, New York. West Publishing Co.

FSD Kenya (2008). The Composition of Public Spending and Growth: Is Current or Capital Spending Better? Oxford Economic Paper, 60, 484–516.Retrieved from 10.1093/oep/gpn005

Ghosh, S., and Gregoriou, A. (2008). The Composition of Government Spending and Growth: Is Current or Capital Spending Better?, *Oxford Economic Papers*, 60(3), 484–516. https://econpapers.repec.org/article/oupoxecpp/v_3a60_3ay_3a2008_3ai_3a3_3ap_3a484-516.htm

Harvard Business Review (2021). Kenya Is Becoming a Global Hub of FinTech Innovation. Retrieved from https://hbr.org/2021/02/kenya-is-becoming-a-global-hub-of-fintech-innovation

Insurance Regulatory Authority (2021a). Mandate, Goals, and National Development Agenda. Retrieved from https://www.ira.go.ke/index.php/about-us/mandate-objectives

Insurance Regulatory Authority (2021b). Licensed Insurance Companies. Retrieved from https://www.ira.go.ke/images/LICENCED-INSURANCE-COMPANIES-2021.pdf

International Monetary Fund (2021). Unemployment Rate. https://www.imf.org/external/datamapper/LUR@WEO/OEMDC/ADVEC/WEOWORLD

Ismail, A.A., Hani, J.I., and Mohammad, M.A. (2020). The Impact of External Environment Factors on Business Continuity Management to Promoting the Higher Education Excellence in Oman. European Journal of Scientific Research. ISSN 1450-216X / 1450-202X Vol. 156 No 3 May, 2020, pp. 327–340 http://www.europeanjournalofscientificresearch.com

Jessop, B. (2002). Liberalism, Neoliberalism, and Urban Governance: A state-theoretical perspective, *International Journal of Urban and Regional Research*, 24, 273–310.

Kenya Law (2012a). Cooperative Societies Act. Chapter 490 of the Laws of Kenya. Retrieved from http://kenyalaw.org/kl/fileadmin/pdfdownloads/Acts/Co-operative-SocietiesActCap490.pdf

Kenya Law (2012b). Capital Markets Authority, Chapter 485A, Laws of Kenya. http://kenyalaw.org:8181/exist/kenyalex/

Kenya Law (2020). National Social Security Fund Act (Chapter 258). Retrieved from http://kenyalaw.org/kl/fileadmin/pdfdownloads/Acts/

Kenya Law (2021). The Constitution of Kenya, 2010(2020) Kenya Law. Retrieved from http://kenyalaw.org/

Kenya National Bureau of Statistics (2020). Economic Survey 2020. Retrieved from https://www.knbs.or.ke/

Kenya National Bureau of Statistics (2021). CPI March 2021. Retrieved from https://www.knbs.or.ke/

Kenya Revenue Authority (2021). Who We Are. Kenya Revenue Authority. Retrieved from https://www.kra.go.ke/en/about-kra

Kenya Vision 2030 (2020). The Third Medium Term Plan 2018–2022. Kenya Vision 2030. Retrieved from http://vision2030.go.ke/publication//

Mauro, P. (1995). Corruption and Growth, *The Quarterly Journal of Economics*, 110(3), August 1995, 681–712, 10.2307/2946696

Mikita, M. (2015). International Monetary Systems: The Desired Direction of Changes. *Procedia Economics and Finance*, 25(2015), 504–510.

Murphy, M.M., Shleifer, A., and Vishny, R.W. (1993). Why is Rent-Seeking Is So Costly to Growth? Retrieved from https://scholar.harvard.edu/shleifer/files/rent_seeking.pdf

Mwega, F.M., and Ndung'u, N.S. (2008). 'Explaining African Economic Growth Performance: The Case of Kenya'. In B.J. Ndulu, S.A. O'Connell, J.-P. Azam, R.H. Bates, A.K. Fosu, J.W. Gunning, and D. Njinkeu (eds), *The Political Economy of Economic Growth in Africa*, 1960–2000. Volume 2: Country Case Studies. Cambridge: Cambridge University Press.

Nairobi Securities Exchange (2021a). Listed Companies. Retrieved from https://www.nse.co.ke/listed-companies/list.html

Nairobi Securities Exchange (2021b). History of NSE. Retrieved from https://www.nse.co.ke/nse/history-of-nse.html

Ndung'u, N.S. (1997). *Price and Exchange Rate Dynamics in Kenya: An Empirical Investigation*, Nairobi Kenya: African Economic Research Consortium. Discussion Paper No. 1.

Njuguna, A.M. and Otsola, J.K. (2011). Predictors of Pension Finance Literacy: A Survey of Members of Occupational Pension Schemes in Kenya International. *Journal of Business and Management*, 6(9); September 2011 10.5539/ijbm.v6n9p101

OECD (2020). Financial System. Retrieved from https://stats.oecd.org/glossary/detail.asp?ID

Republic of Kenya (2019). President Kenyatta Salutes Cooperative Movement, Directs More State Support For SACCOs. PSCU. Retrieved from https://www.president. go.ke/2019/07/20/president-kenyatta-salutes-cooperative-

Republic of Kenya (2020a). Ease of Doing Business – Reform Milestones 2014–2020. Ministry of East Africa Community& Regional Development. Retrieved from https://kenyaembassydc.org/

Republic of Kenya (2020b). Speech by His Excellency Hon Uhuru Kenyatta, During the 2017 Jamhuri Day Celebrations. The Presidency. Retrieved from https://www. president.go.ke/2017/12/12//

Republic of Kenya (2021). 2021 Budget Policy Statement. The National Treasury and Planning. Retrieved from https://www.treasury.go.ke/budget-policy-statement/

Rodrick, D. (2000). *Institutions for High-Quality Growth: What They Are and How to Acquire Them.* Working Paper 7540. National Bureau of Economic Research. 10.3386/w7540

Retirement of Benefits Authority (2021). Types of Schemes. Retrieved from https://www.rba.go.ke/

Simuţ, R. and Meşter, I. (2014). An investigation of cointegration and causality between investments, exports, openness, industrial production and economic growth: A comparative study for the East European countries, Annals of the University of Oradea, *Economic Science Series*, 23(1), 369–378

Special Economic Zones Authority (2021). Investment Opportunities. Retrieved from https://www.sezauthority.go.ke/investment-schemes/industrial-park

Statista (2021). Kenya: National Debt in Relation to Gross Domestic Product from 2016 to 2016. Retrieved from https://www.statista.com/statistics/451122/national-debt-of-kenya-in-relation-to-gross-domestic-product-gdp/

Sultan, Z.A. and Haque, I.M. (2011). The Estimation of the Cointegration Relationship between Growth, Domestic Investment, and Exports: The Indian Economy, *International Journal of Economics and Finance*, 3(4), 226–232.

Tekin, R. (2012). Economic growth, exports and foreign direct investment in Least Developed Countries: A panel Granger causality analysis, *Economic Modelling*, 29, 868–878.

UNCTAD (2008). Services And Development: Implications For The Telecommunications, Banking And Tourism Services Sectors In Kenya. Retrieved from https://unctad.org/system/files/official-document/ditctncd20072_en.pdf

USA State Department (2020). 2020 Investment Climate Statements: Kenya. Retrieved from https://www.state.gov/reports/2020-investment-climate-statements/kenya/

World Bank (2020a). Doing Business 2020: Economy Profile Kenya. Retrieved from https://openknowledge.worldbank.org/bitstream/handle/10986/32436/9781464814402.pdf

World Bank (2020b). Kenya Digital Economy Acceleration Project. Retrieved from https://documents1.worldbank.org/curated/en/175841603290654038/pdf/Concept-Project-Information-Document-PID-Kenya-Digital-Economy-Acceleration-Project-P170941.pdf

World Bank (2020c). Pension and Insurance funds. Retrieved from https://www.worldbank.org/

World Bank (2021a). The World Bank in Africa. Retrieved from https://www.worldbank.org/en/region/afr/overview

World Bank (2021b). Lower Middle Income. Retrieve from https://data.worldbank.org/country/XN

6 Cultural Issues Affecting Business Activity in Kenya

6.1 Introduction

This chapter focuses on culture as a major factor associated with any business development. Both domestic business entrepreneurship and foreign direct investment (FDI) rely on an accurate and proper understanding of how national cultures and subcultures affect the operation of the business in any country. The role of language, national culture and subcultures, religion, and interpersonal communication will be discussed in detail. Kenyan business customs and etiquette will also be examined. Explanations of how culture affects business development will be at the core of this chapter's discussion. As with previous chapters, a major discussion section will focus on why understanding culture as it relates to business development is important.

All societies have a culture comprised of their language, traditions, customs, shared meanings, and institutions. Culture affects everything that happens in any society. It is static and dynamic because culture and its associated behaviors change over time. National cultures and subcultures affect how business is conducted. Culture, language, religion, and interpersonal communication are all important as they influence business customs and etiquette. This chapter directs attention to the different aspects of culture that are important in the Kenyan context. Incorporating all cultural aspects is beyond the scope of this book; therefore, the discussion will be limited to the elements of culture most relevant for entities seeking to do business in Kenya.

The chapter is organized as follows, beginning with a broad definition of culture, followed by introduction of the following topics: (1) subcultures, (2) religion, (3) language and communication patterns (i.e. formal and interpersonal communication) and (4) business etiquette and customs.

6.1.1 Definition of Culture

Geertz Hofstede (1980) presented one of the most popular definitions of culture when he categorized cultures into four dimensions: power distance, uncertainty avoidance, individualism, and masculinity. We will define these four dimensions and compare Kenya with other countries such as the

DOI: 10.4324/9781003095156-6

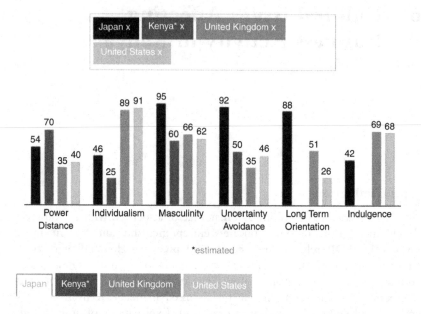

Figure 6.1 Hofstede Cultural Dimensions.

United States, the United Kingdom, and Japan. Figure 6.1 (derived from Hofstede's insights) compares Kenya, the United States, Japan, and the United Kingdom. The selection of the comparison countries is arbitrary, since Hofstede's comparisons are easily accessible. Nonetheless, the authors of this book have collectively spent time in these four selected countries.

6.1.2 Power Distance

Power distance is defined as 'the extent to which less powerful members of organizations and institutions (like the family) accept and expect that power is distributed unequally' (Hofstede & Bond, 1988, p. 10). According to Hofstede, Kenya has a high-power distance culture (score of 70), while the United States has a low power distance culture (score of 40). In practical terms, this means that elders are held in high power distance cultures in high regard. Therefore, older citizens and individuals in positions of power are accorded due respect. Therefore, a company in Kenya needs to know how power distance can influence business interactions. High power distance influences decision-making, especially between junior staff and senior management.

6.1.3 Uncertainty Avoidance

Uncertainty avoidance refers to the degree to which societies can deal with unknown future aspects. Kenya (score of 50) and the United States (score of 46) are both low uncertainty avoidance cultures as compared to Japan (score of 92). This means that individuals in Kenya would be less likely to avoid uncertainty and tend to be less risk-averse compared to the Japanese, implying that Kenya is a great market to introduce new products.

6.1.4 Individualism versus Collectivism

Individualism refers to the 'relationship between the individual and the collectivity which prevails in a given society' (Hofstede, 1980, p. 213). On the individualism scale, Kenya has a collectivistic culture, ranking at 25, while the USA is at 91. In general, the self-concept of most Kenyans is inclusive of their extended family. In his book, *Facing Mount Kenya,* Jomo Kenyatta (1938, p. 213) shares this viewpoint very succinctly, stating:

> According to Gikuyu ways of thinking, nobody is an isolated individual. Or rather his uniqueness is a secondary fact about him: first and foremost, he is several people's relative and several people's contemporary. His life is founded on this fact spiritually and economically, just as much as biologically; the work he does every day is determined by it, and it is the basis of his sense of moral responsibility and social obligation. His personal needs, physical and psychological are satisfied incidentally while he plays his part as a member of a family group, and cannot be fully satisfied in any other way.

While Jomo Kenyatta was discussing the Gikuyu people, this worldview is true of most Kenyan tribes. Thirty-one years later, John Mbiti articulated a similar viewpoint: 'What happens to the individual happens to the whole group, and whatever happens to the whole group happens to the individual.' Mbiti suggested that this is a cardinal point in understanding the African view of humankind. The individual can only say: 'I am because we are; and since we are, therefore I am' (Mbiti, 1969 p. 106). Mbiti also asks,

> what then is the individual and where is his place in the community? In traditional life the individual does not and cannot exist alone except corporately. He owes his existence to other people, including those of past generations and his contemporaries. He is simply part of the whole.
>
> (1969, p. 106)

Kenyans are primarily collectivistic in their orientation, which will undoubtedly affect all aspects of their daily lives. Although individuals vary in their degrees of collectivism versus individualism within Kenyan society, notions of family and group identity are different from group dynamics and identities found in Western countries. Therefore, a company should be well acquainted with these familial relationships when designing protocols such as employment terms and conditions of service (including fringe benefits), different types of leaves, and other family-oriented programs. As such, many Kenyan companies contribute financial resources and accord time off to their employees as they attend 'extended family' obligations. Another commonly accepted practice is family members visiting related employees' workplaces. In other words, the work-family and personal family lines are quite permeable.

6.1.5 Masculinity/Femininity

The masculinity/femininity construct is defined as the degree to which a society is characterized by assertiveness (masculinity) versus nurturance (femininity) (cf. Hofstede, 1980, pp. 262–277). For this scale, Kenya and the United States are rather close, with Kenya ranking as 60 while the United States is at 62. The conclusion here is thus that there will be similarity in levels of assertiveness in Kenya vis a vis the United States, but a marked difference with Japan, which ranks at 95.

6.1.6 Confucian Dynamism and Long-term Orientation versus Indulgence

Hofstede and Bond's subsequent work identified a fifth 'Eastern' dimension, which the authors called 'Confucian dynamism.' Confucian dynamism deals with 'a choice from Confucius' ideas and that its positive pole reflects a dynamic, future-oriented mentality, whereas its negative pole reflects a more static, tradition-oriented mentality' (Hofstede & Bond, 1988, p. 16). Since then, Confucian dynamism has been converted to mean long-term orientation and/or indulgence. At the time of writing, there were no scores available for Kenya for Hofstede's long-term orientation or indulgence; regardless, the United States scored 26, Japan scored 88, and the United Kingdom scored 51. For indulgence, the USA scored 68, Japan scored 42, and the United Kingdom scored 69.

While Hofstede's dimensions are profound for looking at the overall tendencies within a culture, other frameworks are just as important such as those defined by Edward Hall. In 1969, Edward Hall identified two important aspects of culture that are relevant to business: (1) time orientation (m-time versus p-time; and (2) high context versus low context culture, which primarily examines how information is transmitted in different cultures. Because time and information dissemination are very important to business, these two concepts must be developed, discussed, and examined as per their implications in a Kenyan cultural context.

In Hall's seminal book, 'The Silent Language' (1959), he examined time orientation and looked at cultures as either polychronic or monochronic. Monochronic time (M-time) cultures pay attention to one thing at a time, and time is experienced and used linearly. Polychronic time (P-time) means being involved with many things at once. In P-time, many things occur simultaneously as defined by involvement with people. For example, poly-chronic people tend to prioritize human relationships rather than sticking to a schedule. In their personal lives, most Kenyans are polychronic. Edward and Mildred Hall have also stated, 'while we perceive M-time as almost in the air we breathe, it is nevertheless a learned product of northern European culture and is therefore arbitrary and imposed' (1990, p. 14). This imposition is evident in Kenya since many Kenyans keep M-time in their business dealings while operating on P-time in their personal lives. Often, even high-level government meetings start and proceed on P-time.

Interestingly, 'Kenyan time,' which usually refers to P-time, is a real phenomenon. Kenyans are not unique in this regard. This phenomenon has been found in other regions of the world in how local people speak of their goings-on, such as Indian time, Latino time, etc. This does not imply that all Kenyans will be late for meetings but that there are many instances where the Western definition of time and adherence to a schedule will not be prioritized. Despite this observation, non-Kenyan business people are still expected to keep time while doing business in Kenya simply because it is expected of them. They should simultaneously familiarize themselves with P-time if they are to thrive in a Kenyan business environment. With increased Westernization, many Kenyans practice M-time for business transactions and P-time for their personal lives. Coincidentally, Kenyans in the diaspora often maintain this dichotomy in which they adhere to M-time in their professional lives but maintain P-time orientation in their personal lives, especially when dealing with fellow Kenyan Diasporans.

6.1.7 Information

Information dissemination is not the same across cultures. Edward Hall's description of cross-cultural differences can be used to adequately address the concept of information. According to Hall and Hall (1990) cultural differences in information flow are one of the greatest stumbling blocks to international understanding. They suggest that every executive doing business in a different country should be clear about how information is handled and flows, both within the society and within the business. Understandably, there are differences in how information is handled in high-context versus low-context cultures.

6.1.8 High Context versus Low Context Cultures

A high context (HC) communication or message is one in which most of the information is already within the person giving and receiving it, while very little is in the coded, explicit, transmitted part of the message. A low context (LC) communication is just the opposite; i.e. the mass of the information is vested in the explicit code (Hall, 1976, p. 91, as quoted in Hall 1990, p. 6). Kenya is regarded as a HC culture, unlike the LC United States. Meyer (2014, p. 40) has noted that most HC cultures have a long-shared history and are usually relationship-oriented societies where networks of connections are passed from generation to generation, creating more shared context among community members. On the other hand, a low-context culture such as the United States has a shorter shared history and, as a nation of immigrants, has little shared context. Meyers suggests that Americans have learned to communicate explicitly and clearly to leave little room for ambiguity and misunderstanding. This difference in how information is transmitted has major implications for business transactions. For example, when meetings are held in high-context cultures, everything needs to be spelled out in an agenda, whereas in low-context cultures, items not on the agenda can be discussed.

6.1.9 Summary of Definition

The prior section introduced historical definitions of culture, which have been applied to the Kenyan context. The focus in this section relates to subcultures, or tribes, in Kenya. While much of the rest of the world is fascinated with African tribal systems and, in recent years, has tried to move toward from the use of the term 'ethnic group' rather than refer to tribes as tribes, Africans on the continent do not hold the same negative attitude toward the word 'tribe.' Indeed, many Africans, and as a consequence, many Kenyans, not only know what a tribe is, but they are also historically connected to a 'tribe.' In some cases, this impedes nation-building because of allegiance to tribe over the country. Throughout Africa, national governments continue to work toward building a common identity based on nationhood rather than on tribal membership. The Kenyan government has worked diligently to build a sense of one Kenya with no tribal emphasis i.e. a 'One Kenya, One Tribe' philosophy. Despite these efforts, no examination of Kenyan culture would be complete without a basic understanding of tribal systems and their importance.

6.2 National Culture and Subcultures

According to the 2020 Kenya Census, there are 45 tribes in the country. The CIA Factbook (2021) states that the dominant tribes in Kenya are as follows: Kikuyu 17.1 percent, Luhya 14.3 percent, Kalenjin 13.4 percent, Luo 10.7 percent, Kamba 9.8 percent, Somali 5.8 percent, Kisii 5.7 percent, Mijikenda 5.2 percent, Meru 4.2 percent, Maasai 2.5 percent, Turkana 2.1 percent, non-Kenyan 1 percent and other tribes constitute 8.2 percent (2019 est.) Because of Kenya's colonial history, there are a significant number of Indian Kenyans whose ancestry dates back to British Colonial rule. During the colonial era, Indians operated small businesses, served in the British Army in East Africa, and worked on constructing the Kenya-Ugandan Railway (Ombur, 2017). In July 21, 2017, Kenya's acting minister of the interior, Fred Matiang'i, announced that Kenyans of Indian descent would now be categorized as the 44th Kenyan tribe (see Ombur, 2017). Indian Kenyans have historically been involved in many business enterprises, including manufacturing. Any company doing business in Kenya would immediately learn of the important role that Indian Kenyans have played in the Kenyan economy.

While the majority of Indians in Kenya originated from Southeast Asia, the rest of the Kenyan tribes stem from a specific region in the country. Each of the tribes has an ancestral origin, and tribal members share similar language, food, music and cultural practices. Generally, one's tribe can often be inferred from their name or region of origin in Kenya. In most regions, most people who live in that region are usually from the same tribe and often speak the same language. The exception to this rule is urban areas such as Nairobi, Nakuru, Mombasa, Eldoret, Kisumu, etc., where people from the rest of the country congregate in search of employment and investment opportunities. One's tribe influences many aspects of a person's life since many people are born into a given tribe. While tribal allegiance is slowly dissipating in Kenya due to intermarriages and urban life, one's tribe is still very important. A close examination of politics and other aspects of social life shows that adherence to one's tribal practices is still very pervasive. The non-tribal future looks bright since many young educated Kenyans marry across different tribes. Many also do not speak the tribal language of their parents and in many cases, do not espouse their associated tribal values. Nonetheless, it would be erroneous for any company in Kenya to ignore the importance of tribal ties. Moreover, investors need to acquire knowledge beyond superficial knowledge about the concept of tribes and their impact when conducting business in Kenya and in many parts of Africa.

Tribal politics and knowledge are even more important in Kenya because a feature unique to Kenyan tribes is that most of them have their own media in the form of radio and TV stations. Many YouTubers provide content in their tribal languages, then broadcast it throughout their region. Therefore, placing advertisements on local language TV stations, YouTube channels or radio stations is essential when promoting goods and services. As such, advertising campaigns in different geographical regions would necessitate hiring locals who speak the local language.

6.3 Languages

According to the Kenyan Embassy in the United States, there are over 42 different languages spoken in Kenya. English, the official language, is used in school instruction, business transactions, and government operations. The national language of Kenya is Kiswahili, and almost every Kenyan speaks it. Over 100 million people speak Kiswahili in East and Central Africa. While English is the language of instruction in schools, most Kenyans learn Kiswahili in elementary school. Hence, most educated Kenyans speak a minimum of three languages – English, Kiswahili, and their tribal language. Moreover, most young people speak a derivation of English, Kiswahili, and other local languages called Sheng. Githinji (2006, p. 444) defines Sheng as, 'an acronym for Swahili-English slang' e.g. (Mazrui, 1995) and is 'a hybrid linguistic code that is believed to have evolved in Nairobi in the 1960s to 1970s.' What is distinctive about Sheng is that there is no standard Sheng language. Because it is formed/derived in the urban settings where it is most spoken, it is continuously evolving, and different regions have different versions of Sheng. Nairobi, the capital city, generates most of the language. Githinji has also noted:

> Today Sheng has become a characteristic linguistic phenomenon of Nairobi and other multiethnic urban areas in Kenya, though the degree of competence and participation differ from individual to individual among different categories of speakers.
>
> (2006, p. 445)

The frequent use of Sheng in business, particularly in advertising, has been studied by scholars such as Mutonya (2008), who examined advertisements in print and electronic media. Mutonya (2008, p. 8) noted that Sheng and non-standard forms in multilingual Swahili ads have effectively articulated the new fluid and multiple identities of a growing city, facilitated the redefinition of existing social and linguistic boundaries and served as an effective face-saving tool in broaching sensitive national issues. Understanding Sheng and its role in business is necessary for a company to succeed in Kenya. Likewise, a company doing business in Kenya must understand the different languages its employees and customers speak. This is increasingly true since most Kenyans use code switching (English at work, Swahili at work, and in other contexts, tribal languages). Okamura (1981, p. 452) indicated that Kenyans display situational ethnicity. As early as 1967, Paden suggested that 'situational ethnicity is premised on the observation that particular contexts may determine which of a person's communal identities or loyalties are appropriate at a point in time' (Paden, 1967). Researchers such as Stayman and Deshpande (1989) have also examined situational ethnicity.

6.4 Gender Norms

The USAID data (2020) indicates that Kenya scores 81 (out of 100) on the Women, Business and the Law 2020 index, ranking 109 out of 153 countries in the Global Gender Gap Report 2020 with a score of 0.671. Significant inequalities between males and females in education, health outcomes, representation in public leadership positions, and participation in the labor market remain. In the recent past, however, the Kenyan government has instituted legislative and policy reforms to establish a basis for gender equality across all sectors. Gender equality and non-discrimination are UN-based developmental goals guaranteed in the Kenyan Constitution of 2010. Kenya's Vision 2030 seeks to mainstream gender equality in all aspects of society (Kenya National Bureau of Statistics – Gender Sector Statistics Plan, December 2020).

Kenya is also a signatory to several international treaties and conventions that recognize the full equality of women. While full equality has not yet been realized, women in Kenya have made many strides in equality in many sectors. For example, the 2010 Kenyan Constitution Article 27(8) of the Bill of Rights states that: 'State shall take legislative and other measures to implement the principle that not more than two-thirds of the members of elective or appointive bodies shall be of the same gender.' As of 2019, women represented 22 percent of all elected positions in the national assembly and 18 percent of the nominated positions. In the Senate, women held 27 percent of all elected positions and 86 percent of the nominated positions. Within the county assembly, 34 percent of all members were women. A study by the International Center for Research on Women, in conjunction with the Kenya Association of Manufacturers, found that most women-owned manufacturing businesses are micro, small, and medium-sized enterprises (MSMEs) operating in the informal sector (Mugyenyi et al., 2020). They further found that although women-owned MSMEs comprised 20 percent of Kenya's GDP, many are unable to grow into medium-sized enterprises since they experience high costs of production, transport, and capital outlay.

Kenya has attained impressive literacy rates in the education sector – 85 percent among men and 78.2 percent among women. In comparison, Tanzania has 83.1 percent for men and 73.1 percent for women, while in Uganda, literacy rates for men are 82.7 percent and 70.8 percent for women. With increased education comes increased economic empowerment. Additionally, as women become more educated, they have more agency concerning the number of desired children. This resulted in lower fertility rates (3.36 children per woman) compared to 1972 when fertility rates stood at 7.3 children per woman.

This progress notwithstanding, Kenya is still a very patriarchal society, and women are disenfranchised in many spheres of life in which they hold subservient positions. Many women and adolescent girls are still vulnerable due to harmful cultural norms, as well as economic and educational disparities that lead to higher poverty. Figure 6.2 shows the gender inequality index across five East African countries. Among these five countries, Rwanda ranks the lowest in gender inequality due to national government policies. Ironically, Kenya has the highest gender inequality among the five countries.

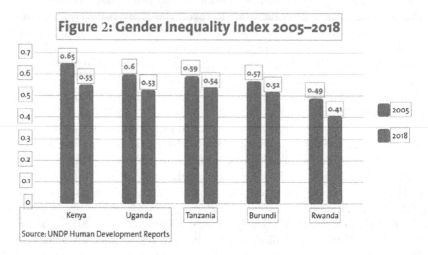

Figure 6.2 Gender Inequality Index 2005–2018.

6.5 Family Definition

In many Western contexts, the definition of family includes a smaller subset of people than in most African contexts. In his classic work, *African Religions and Philosophy*, John Mbithi (1969) highlighted this difference:

> For African peoples, the family has a much wider circle of members than the word suggests in Europe or North America. In traditional society, the family includes, children, parents, grandparents, uncles, aunts, brothers and sisters who may have their own children, and other immediate relatives.
>
> (Mbiti, 1969, p. 104)

Family ties as a function of marriage also extend this definition of family. Jomo Kenyatta wrote about marriage as 'the linking of two families in bonds which are social and economic as well as biological, and which are, in fact, the connecting links of tribal life' (1938, p. 217). These families work as a unit, with intricate obligations to both the biological family and the married family, especially during marriages, funerals and other life-defining moments. It is common practice that when employees wed, co-workers and the company give sizable gifts to the bride and groom. Marriage is highly valued and bestows honor and respect on the persons who enter into the institution.

Additionally, during funerals, it is the norm that co-workers and the company provide financial resources to support the bereaved employee. Therefore, a company doing business in Kenya needs to adequately understand the definition of family, which goes beyond the cursory knowledge of nuclear versus extended family. Finally, in terms of family relationships, filial responsibility/duty has historically been deeply ingrained in the psyche of most Kenyans. Kenyans from all walks of life are commonly intimately involved in caring for their elderly parents. As such, few to non-existent elderly care homes are available in Kenya. On the other hand, Kenya has a very young population, with a median age of 19.9 years for males and 20.1 for females. The life expectancy has been increasing and currently stands at 69.32 years for the total population, with 67.5 years for males and 71.03 years for females.

6.6 Role of Religion

The majority of Kenyans practice some type or form of religion. The major religions are Christianity, Islam, and Hinduism, while many also practice African religions. The CIA Factbook (2019) estimates the religious demographics in Kenya as Christian 85.5 percent (comprised of Protestant 33.4 percent, Catholic 20.6 percent, Evangelical 20.4 percent, African Instituted Churches 7 percent, other Christian 4.1 percent); Muslims account for 10.9 percent, and the rest are other 1.8 percent, none 1.6 percent, don't know/no answer 0.2 percent. With 85 percent of Kenyans practicing Christianity, many Kenyans attend church services on Sundays.

Most businesses and government offices are closed during the weekend. In addition, the observance of Friday as a day for prayers among Kenyan Muslims is valued by practitioners of Islam. Among the recognized Kenyan public holidays are the Christian holidays of Easter Monday, Good Friday, and Christmas Day, the Islamic holidays of Eid al-Fitr and Eid al-Adha, and the Hindu holiday of Deepavali. Religion, therefore, affects many aspects of life in Kenya. In marriage and death, for example, one's religion influences how matters proceed. Sharia law applies to Muslim marriages; tribal customs govern African customary marriages, Christian traditions govern Christian marriagestraditions, and Hindu marriages are governed by Hindu traditions. Civil marriages are officiated by a registrar of marriages in the Office of the Attorney General and Department of Justice. Another area where religion is relevant is in the education sector. Many schools teach not only the standard curriculum but also the faith of a particular sect. In Kenya, children can matriculate in Hindu schools, Muslim schools, Catholic schools, and Evangelical schools, among many others.

Because of the country's religious plurality, Kenyans are generally exposed to and comfortable with many different religions. Even within families, members might practice different religious faiths, particularly given where they went to school. Evangelical Christians have seen the biggest rise in membership in recent years, with many new mega-churches built in different regions of the country. Finally, while most Kenyans practice Christianity, Islam, or Hinduism, many also have metaphysical beliefs that align with African religious practices. In Kenya, there has been a rise in the number of people practicing African indigenous religions. Despite conversion to the religions mentioned above, African religions are not extinct. John Mbiti (as quoted by Burleson, 1986, p. 12), when analyzing statistics of African conversion to Islam or Christianity, suggested that Africans 'come out of African religion, but they don't take off their traditional religiosity. They come as they are. They come as a people whose world view is shaped according to African religion.' In his book on *African Religion the Moral Traditions of Abundant Life,* Laurenti Magesa (1998: 20) writes:

> Much as they might want to deny it at times, this dual thought-system noted by scholars still influences many Western - "educated" Africans, who show their true African religious face particularly in times of crisis. Many African professors, ministers of government and members of parliament have been known to "revert" in secret to the diviner or medium in order to know what lies ahead while at the same time vigorously protesting in public that diviners are relics of bygone "primitive" times and that they possess no mystical powers ... . Christianity in Africa today may be said to have two different forms of thought-systems and faith expressions - one official and one popular. Official Christianity is the faith expression that is promulgated in the seminaries and other centers of training, as well as in sermons and homilies by various pastoral agents. The vast majority of Christian faithful, however, appropriate the teaching of the official church according to their own circumstances and needs using the dominant symbol system of African religion.

6.7 Dynamics of Interpersonal Communication

As mentioned earlier, Kenya is a high-context culture; therefore, Kenyan people are expected to be more implicit than explicit in their communication. In describing the differences between cultures that are explicit (i.e., the United States and other Anglo-Saxon cultures in which people are trained (mostly subconsciously) to communicate as literally and explicitly as possible) and implicit cultures, like African cultures, Meyer (2014, p. 31) has stated that 'Good communication is subtle, layered, and may depend on copious subtext, with responsibility for transmission of the message shared between the one sending the message and the one receiving it.' This is in contrast to other cultures, where 'Good communication is about clarity and explicitness, and accountability for accurate transmission of the message is placed firmly on the communicator: "If you don't understand it's my fault."' Meyer also claimed that this type of implicit communication was found in Asian cultures such as India, China, Japan and Indonesia; in African cultures such as Kenya and Zimbabwe; and Latin American cultures and Latin European cultures. Verbal and nonverbal communication has certain particularities in Kenya.

6.7.1 Verbal Communication

Kenyans are generally indirect communicators who are polite and friendly. Because they come from a high power distance culture, they respect hierarchy and often defer to elders and their superiors. Saving face is important for Kenyans, so criticism is often delivered privately to save face.

6.7.2 Non-verbal Communication

Personal space is much closer than in most Western contexts; however, physical contact and public displays of affection are minimal. Public displays of affection occasionally appear in urban settings, especially among young people. Interestingly, people of the same gender holding hands without being in a romantic relationship is common in Kenya. Another cultural difference in non-verbal communication is that it is normal to wave all fingers of one hand rather than use one finger when beckoning someone. In most urban settings, people make eye contact, but in rural areas, people may not make eye contact with those who are their superiors or elders. Furthermore, when visiting people, especially in their homes, accepting any hospitality offers, such as tea, coffee, or some food, is expected.

Technology has had an important impact on interpersonal communication (Berger, 2013), as evidenced by the impact that Facebook, Twitter, and email have had on communication. According to Berger (2013, p. 1), communication over the Internet differs because it is written, undirected, anonymous, and involves larger audiences with a reduced social presence compared to face-to-facecommunication. According to Internet World Stats, over 85 percent of Kenyans regularly use the internet. The most popular app of choice for communication is WhatsApp – in 2020, Kenya led the world with 97 percent WhatsApp penetration rates. Most Kenyans belong to multiple WhatsApp groups, family groups, neighborhood groups, work groups, religious groups, and even ad-hoc groups. Most Kenyans, including the authors, have inadvertently been added to many WhatsApp groups. In addition, Kenyans are prolific social media users, with 8.8 million in Kenya as of January 2020 (Kemp, 2020).

6.8 Values and Attitudes

In Kenya, there is no single overarching value system because of the many different tribes. In this chapter, values such as individualism versus collectivism; power distance; uncertainty avoidance; time orientation; gender egalitarianism; assertiveness (i.e., the masculinity-femininity index); high context versus low context culture; and attitudes toward time, family, and the elderly have been compared and contrasted, as well as examining how all of these values intersect with everyday life and ultimately impact how business is conducted. The discussion of all values is beyond the scope of this chapter. The topics and values discussed in this chapter are designed to reveal relevant cultural values and practices.

6.9 Role of Education

As mentioned earlier in the chapter, Kenya has invested heavily in education, resulting in high literacy rates. Kenya has had free and compulsory primary education since January 6, 2003, consistent with the Millennium Development Goals. Free primary education aims to ensure that all Kenyan children receive a primary education without discrimination. The transition from primary to secondary education has been impressive and currently stands at 100 percent for 2020 Kenya Certificate of Primary Education (KCPE) candidates. Speaking to the media about the KCPE 2020 results, Professor George Magoha, the Cabinet Secretary for Education, said, 'All candidates will transition to secondary schools, and the Ministry of Education has already conducted an audit of vacancies in both private and public secondary schools' (as quoted in Vidija and Too 2021). The transition to secondary schools has been made possible by changes in government policy. In 2008, the Kenyan government instituted subsidized free-day secondary education (SFDSE). The goal of SFDSE was to reduce the cost burden on parents and to enable more children access to the minimum basic secondary education (Asena et al., 2016).

Concerning higher education, there were eight universities in Kenya before 2008. The Universities Act, established in 2012, provided the authority to develop more institutions of higher learning. It also provided accreditation and governance for universities. As of 2021, there are 24 public and 27 private universities in Kenya. Furthermore, the majority of these universities have campuses in more than one part of the country.

Consequently, there are many opportunities for young people in Kenya to pursue higher education. Nonetheless, the government is working vigorously to ensure that all county children have access to education. In some parts of Kenya, especially in communities that have prioritized the education of boys over girls for various cultural reasons, there has been a big push to prioritize the 'girl child,' and the fruits of these efforts are becoming more evident over time. There is a common saying that when a girl is educated, the whole village is educated because educated women have children who value education. Moreover, the more educated women are in a community, the more development-focused they are, so the overall community benefits.

Culturally, Kenyans value education as a means of economic empowerment and social mobility. Therefore, parents spend a significant portion of their income educating their children to secure success. Education is highly valued, and those who hold advanced degrees or advanced education are accorded community respect. It is a status symbol for parents to have their children educated at a university level. In many communities, many people are among the first generation of university graduates in their families. Coincidentally, this is true for two of the authors of this book, providing clear anecdotal evidence of the transformative power of education.

Companies should care about education in Kenya because education ensures a ready and educated workforce. Education offers a variety of business skill sets and competencies needed in contemporary business environments. Many companies in Kenya are involved in corporate social responsibility (CSR) efforts that directly impact education. For example, Kenya Equity Bank, through its 'Wings to Fly Scholarship,' provides comprehensive secondary school scholarships to academically promising and financially disadvantaged youth. Furthermore, the Equity Leaders Program provides professional and leadership development opportunities for top performers who attend leading local and global universities. Deloitte East Africa, McKinsey & Company, Mastercard Foundation, and the Coca-Cola Foundation are other companies partnered with USAID and other institutions to provide education access as part of their CSR. Tuition assistance and reimbursement are also common employee benefits provided by employers.

6.10 Business Customs and Etiquette

Generally, business environments promote a set of rules that govern the way people interact with one another. Most Kenyan business meetings start with greetings and usual handshakes with everyone present. Meetings and negotiations are primarily conducted in English. Small talk is expected at the beginning of meetings, and formal business dress is expected (suits for men and dresses or suits for women). In 2019, the government ordered all civil servants to wear 'Made in Kenya' clothing on Fridays (see Komu, 2019, Nairobi News). Kenyans tend to be very formal in business meetings and use titles liberally. Even outside of the work environment, people will be referred to by their job titles such as engineer, professor, doctor, lawyer, etc.

Hierarchy is also important, given that Kenya is a high-power distance country. Consequently, individuals in positions of power are accorded tremendous respect, while people in subordinate positions know their place in the hierarchy and conduct themselves accordingly. Negotiations are carried out for most transactions. In fact, in most places outside of supermarkets, bargaining is part of the culture. Business cards are exchanged easily in business settings, although there are no clear guidelines about who hands over their business card first. As far as gift-giving is concerned, many companies give calendars and diaries/appointment books as corporate marketing items, particularly at the end of the calendar year. When co-workers face challenges, such as sickness or death of a loved one, or experience happy occasions, such as weddings and births, co-workers contribute money in line with the concept of Harambee ('let us pull together') to support their co-workers.

Participation in these events is optional but indirectly required if one is to thrive and get along with others in the work environment and social settings. One remnant of British culture is that tea is served or is available in offices at 10 am and 4 pm. The working day usually starts from 8:00 am to 5 pm, with an hour for lunch. Many businesses are closed during the lunch hour and on weekends.

6.11 Discussion and Conclusion

This chapter has highlighted the different cultural elements one would need to be familiar with when doing business in Kenya. Importantly, these cultural tendencies are not present in every person. Nonetheless, there are important cultural considerations for successful business in Kenya, so getting cultural nuances right can distinguish one company from another. As this chapter concludes, the fact that Kenyans, and especially educated Kenyans, straddle traditional African values and Western modern values should be underscored. As highlighted before, Kenyans display situational ethnicity in most life domains. While a Kenyan may be comfortable eating and consuming Western food while wearing Western dress, they are most likely still deeply rooted in their traditional beliefs. This is evidenced by the foods they consume, the clothing they wear and, even more importantly, the way they celebrate many rites of passage.

Kenya has a beautiful and rich culture, and companies doing business in Kenya have an opportunity to experience many different cultural practices in a cosmopolitan, highly technologically advanced environment. Indeed, one does not have to veer too far from the main urban areas to experience the beauty of the many cultures in this country. From the nomadic, pastoral tribes like the Maasai to the land dwellers (Kikuyus and Kisii's), or the coastal tribes, there is enough culture, beauty, and diversity of experiences to enjoy and take advantage of within a short distance of Nairobi, Mombasa Kisumu or Eldoret, the main cities.

References

Berger, J. (2013). Beyond Viral: Interpersonal Communication in the Internet Age, *Psychological Inquiry*, 24, 293–296, Doi: 10.1080/1047840X.2013.842203

Burleson, B.W. (1986). *John Mbiti: The Dialogue of an African Theologian with African Traditional Religion*, Dissertation Thesis, Baylor University.

Cia factbook, https://www.cia.gov/the-world-factbook/countries/kenya/ retrieved April 21, 2021.

Equity Bank, https://equitygroupfoundation.com/wings-to-fly/ retrieved April 20, 2021.

Githinji, P. (2006). Bazes and Their Shibboleths: Lexical Variation and Sheng Speakers' Identity in Nairobi, *Nordic Journal of African Studies*, 15(4), 443–472.

Hofstede Insights, https://www.hofstede-insights.com/product/compare-countries/ Retrieved April 20, 2021.

Hall, E.T. (1959). *The Silent Language*, Garden City, New York: Doubleday & Company, Inc.

Hall, E.T. (1966). *The Hidden Dimension*, Garden City, New York: Doubleday & Company Inc.

Hall, E.T. (1976). *Beyond Culture*, New York: Anchor Press/Doubleday.

Hall, E.T. and Hall, M. (1990). *Understanding Cultural Differences*, Yarmouth, Maine: Intercultural Press, Inc.

Hofstede, G.H. (1980). *Culture's Consequences*, Beverly Hills, CA: Sage Publications.

Hofstede, G.H. and Bond, M.H. (1988). The Confucius Connection, from Cultural Roots to Economic Growth, *Organizational Dynamics*, 16(4), 5–21.

https://www.knbs.or.ke/?wpdmpro=gender-sector-statistics-plan, Retrieved April 19, 2021.

https://www.standardmedia.co.ke/kenya/article/2001409784/2020-kcpe-results-out retrieved April 19, 2021.

Internet World Stats (2020). Internet penetration in Africa 2020 – Q1 – March, https://www.internetworldstats.com/stats1.htm, retrieved April 22, 2021.

James, A.M.S., Mukasa, A., and Riechi, A. (2016). Factors Affecting Subsidized Free Day Secondary Education in Enhancing Learners Retention in Secondary Schools in Kenya, *Journal of Education and Practice*, 7(20), 2016, 49–55.

Kemp, Simon (2020). Digital 2020: Kenya, https://datareportal.com/reports/digital-2020-kenya Retrieved April 22nd 2021.

Kenyan Embassy-USA "About Kenya – Culture" https://kenyaembassydc.org/aboutkenyaculture/ Retrieved, April 21st 2021.

Kenya National Bureau of Statistics – UN Gender Sector Statistics Plan: December 2020.

Kenyatta, J. (1938). *Facing Mt. Kenya*, Nairobi, Kenya: Printwell Industries.

Komu, N. (2019). Govt orders all civil servants to wear 'Made in Kenya' on Fridays, https://nairobinews.nation.co.ke/featured/govt-orders-all-civil-servants-to-wear-made-in-kenya-on-fridays, retrieved April 21, 2021.

Kwach, J. (2019). List of tribes in Kenya, https://www.tuko.co.ke/281554-list-tribes-kenya.html, retrieved April 22, 2021.

Laurenti, M. (1998). *African Religion the Moral Traditions of Abundant Life*, Nairobi, Kenya: Paulines Publications Africa/Daughters of St Paul.

Mazrui, A.A.A. (1974). *World Culture and the Black Experience*, Seattle and London: University of Washington Press.

Mazrui, A. (1995). Slang and Codeswitching: The case of Sheng in Kenya, *Afrikanistische Arbeitspapiere*, 42, 168–179.

Meyer, E. (2014). *The Culture Map: Breaking through the Invisible Boundaries of Global Business*, New York, NY: Public Affairs.

Mbiti, J.S. (1969) *African Religions and Philosophy*, Garden City, New York: AnchoBooks Doubleday & Company, Inc.

Mugyenyi, C., Nduta, N., Ajema, C., Afifu, C., Yegon, E. (2020). Women in Manufacturing: Mainstreaming Gender and Inclusion in Kenya, report by International Center for Research on Women and Kenya Association of Manufacturers. https://www.icrw.org/publications/women-in-manufacturing-mainstreaming-gender-and-inclusion-in-kenya/, retrieved April 22, 2021.

Mutonya, M. (2008). Swahili advertising in Nairobi: innovation and language shift, *Journal of African Cultural Studies*, 20, 1, June, 3–14.

Mwaniki, M.K. (1973). *The Relationship Between Self-concept and Academic Achievement in Kenyan Pupils*. Unpublished doctoral dissertation, Stanford: CA: Stanford University.

Okamura, J.Y. (1981). Situational Ethnicity, *Ethnic and Racial Studies*, 4(October), 452–465.

Ombur, Rael (2017). Kenyans of Asian Descent Become Nation's 44th Tribe retrieved April 16, 2021. https://www.voanews.com/africa/kenyans-asian-descent-become-nations-44th-tribe

Paden, J.N. (1967). Situational Ethnicity in Urban Africa with Special Reference to the Hausa. Paper presented at *African Studies Association Meeting* in New York, November.

Patrick, V. and Too, J. (2021). 2020 KCPE results announced. Standard, April 15, 2021.

Stayman, D., Deshpande, M.R. (1989). Situational Ethnicity and Consumer Behavior, *Journal of Consumer Research*, 16(3), December, 361–371. 10.1086/209222

USAID (2020). Gender Equality and Female Employment in Kenya, https://www.usaid.gov/documents/1860/support-gender-equality-kenya-fact-sheet, retrieved April 18, 2021

7   Establishing Business in Kenya

7.1 Introduction

Kenya is an attractive market in which to invest, and the Kenyan government has focused on easing the process of doing business in the country. Kenya was ranked eighth in Africa as one of the best countries for business by Forbes 2019 (Ecofin Agency 2019). In 2015, the Kenyan government revised the 1948 Companies Act, which favored larger businesses. The new Act was designed to support small- and medium-sized businesses. In 2018, the Kenyan government established the Department of Business Reforms and Transformation (DBRT). The DBRT was mandated to implement business reforms across all levels and all arms of government. These reforms were designed to make Kenya more competitive in local and international markets. All of these efforts have paid off, making Kenya an attractive market in which to invest. In 2018, CITI Research found Kenya to have the highest mobile money penetration globally. In 2019, PricewaterhouseCoopers (PwC) ranked Kenya first as the leading business destination in Africa for large companies looking for growth prospects (Deca, 2020). In 2019, Kenya was ranked 56th globally for its Ease of Doing Business in the World's Doing Business report. By 2022, the Kenyan government intends to rank in the top 20 on the Ease of Doing Business rankings. Furthermore, the World Bank ranked Kenya first globally in protecting minority shareholders/investors, and it ranked Kenya fourth globally on access to credit.

The following sections will focus on important aspects of starting a business in Kenya. It is not possible to comprehensively cover all aspects; therefore, we will only cover the most important areas of establishing a business. It is noteworthy that in all countries, government regulations and policies change in response to the domestic and global environment. Therefore, we will point the reader to available resources for the most up-to-date information. The Kenyan government has invested heavily in online portals that have made the registration of businesses expeditious and efficient. Online registration has increased the number of companies being registered annually. For example, in 2020, 200 companies were registered daily for a total of 400,00 businesses. Additionally, it only takes one day for customs documentary compliance,

DOI: 10.4324/9781003095156-7

down from seven days due to automation (Ease of Doing Business, p. 8). Further, in the period 2020–2021, the Kenyan government, through the DBRT, implemented major reforms in the following areas: registering a company, obtaining plan approvals, accessing electricity, registering property, paying taxes, importing and exporting processes, accessing justice for businesses, including business restructuring and insolvency, and procuring public and legal reforms (see. https://brs.go.ke/assets/downloads/Kenya-Business-Climate-Reforms-Milestone-Report-2020-2021.pdf).

7.1.1 Attractiveness of Kenya

Kenya has a unique advantage because it has abundant educated human capital. Between 2015–2019, Kenya ranked fourth in Africa and 94th globally in the Human Capital Index. Kenya has a very young population. The median age is 20 years, and 59.16 percent of the population is 24 years and under (Cia Factbook). In addition, Kenya's literacy rate is 81.5 percent for the total population, 85 percent for males, and 78.2 percent for females. This is one of the highest literacy rates in Sub-Saharan Africa.

Furthermore, Kenyans are very entrepreneurial, and many organizations, such as Nailab, Chandaria Business Innovation, and Incubation Center, support innovation and entrepreneurship. Sam Gichuru, Nailab's founder, describes what these organizations do: "We are providing a platform where startup entrepreneurs can leverage on technology, knowledge, and funding opportunities to solve problems facing emerging markets"(Nailab website). Comparing South African entrepreneurs to Kenyan entrepreneurs, South African millionaire Vusi Thembekwayo in a 2016 article, noted that Kenya has strong social systems that reward entrepreneurs with social status and support when they have business ideas. In his article on business ideas in Africa, Vincent Nyoike describes some of the best business incubators in Kenya for entrepreneurs (Nyoike).

7.1.2 Challenges of Investing in Kenya

Although the investment climate in Kenya is excellent, corruption has been identified as an impediment to business. In 2021, Kenya scored 30 out of 100 in Transparency International's Global Corruption Perceptions Index, where a score of zero means highly corrupt and 100 was very clean. Additionally, out of 180 countries, Kenya ranked 128th which is close to the bottom of the list. Like most other countries, the coronavirus pandemic negatively impacted investment and economic opportunities in the short term. Still, the government has been applauded for handling current economic and health challenges (export.gov). There is high unemployment among the youth (currently at 7.2 percent), which was exacerbated by the Covid-19 shutdown (Youth Unemployment, 2022). Other factors influencing business are heightened levels of insecurity, poverty, ethnic tensions, and land ownership issues.

2019 Procedures

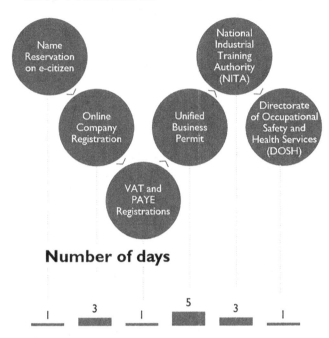

Figure 7.1 2019 Procedures of Starting a Business.
Source: Ease of Doing Business Report 2019.

7.2 Investment in New Business Venture

To register a company in Kenya, foreign companies must file with the registrar of companies by following the steps outlined below (Figure 7.1).

The registration process has been streamlined by automation. To register a company, one must visit the e-Citizen portal (https://www.ecitizen.go.ke/ecitizen-services.html), which is the gateway for all government services. At the e-Citizen portal a company can submit three preferred names and pay registration fees, which were substantially reduced in 2020. A company can also access all the documents needed to establish a business. Moreover, it is now possible for a company to obtain an electronic certificate of incorporation, a Kenya Revenue Authority Personal Identification Number (KRA PIN), Pay as you Earn (PAYE), Value Added Tax (VAT), National Hospital Insurance Fund (NHIF), and National Social Security Fund (NSSF) as part of online registration. Efficient and shortened registration times have saved applicants a lot of time.

7.3 Entities and Licensing

When establishing a business, individuals must deal with numerous agencies; therefore, we will focus on the most critical areas. Since businesses vary in the operating licenses, we only focus on the most basic licenses. For company-specific requirements, the reader is advised to consult the Kenya investment website and other resources listed at the end of this chapter. In the following section, we describe government agencies, parastatals, and other private sector entities that facilitate conducting business in Kenya.

7.3.1 Government and Private Entities

When establishing a business in Kenya, potential investors should be aware of various acts that govern business and the myriad organizations and legislative bodies that impact business.

1   Kenya Revenue Authority (KRA) was established in 1995 through an Act of Parliament to collect individual and business taxes for the Kenyan government. KRA offers fiscal (tax) incentives, such as capital, industrial, and investment deductions. Moreover, Export Processing Zone (EPZ) projects receive fiscal and many other benefits (https://www.kra.go.ke/en/about-kra).

2   National Social Security Fund (NSSF) was established in 1965 by an Act of Parliament to provide social security benefits to Kenyans upon retirement. When it was first established, it offered a pension and a provident fund (https://www.nssf.or.ke/).

3   National Hospital Insurance Fund (NHIF) is a parastatal organization established in 1966 by an Act of Parliament to provide medical insurance to all members and their dependents. At 18, any Kenyan can become a member of NHIF (http://www.nhif.or.ke/healthinsurance/).

4   National Environment Management Authority (NEMA) was established in 1999 as the principal government instrument in implementing all environmental policies. NEMA ensures sustainable management of the environment by exercising general supervision and coordination over all matters relating to the environment (https://www.nema.go.ke/).

5   The Kenya Investment Authority (KenInvest) was established in 2004 to promote investments, facilitate investments, and provide after-investment care to ensure that investment projects are implemented without problems. To invest in Kenya, an investor must obtain an investment certificate that qualifies them as an investor. KenInvest can assist individual investors individuals in obtaining an investment certificate http://www.invest.go.ke/who-we-are/.

6   Kenya National Chamber of Commerce and Industry (KNCCI) is a not-for-profit company established to facilitate and promote a sustainable business environment for economic growth and prosperity. KNCCI is a

membership organization comprised of small, micro, medium, and large enterprises, and it protects the commercial and industrial interests of the business community (https://www.kenyachamber.or.ke/about-kncci/).

7 Kenya Private Sector Alliance (KEPSA), which was established in 2003 and is a limited liability membership organization, is comprised of many different organizations and represents more than one million businesses that collectively lobby the government, development partners, and relevant stakeholders on matters affecting the private sector (https://kepsa.or.ke/).

8 Federation of Kenya Employers (FKE) was established in 1959 under the Trade Unions Act to represent the interests of local as well as international employers. It is the most representative employers' organization in Kenya (https://www.fke-kenya.org/).

9 Kenya Association of Manufacturers (KAM) represents manufacturing and value-added industries in Kenya. KAM partners with the government and other agencies in order to ensure world-class, competitive and sustainable local manufacturing (https://kam.co.ke/).

10 Kenya Investment Authority provides a one-stop resource for all investment-related questions such as starting a business, providing services to investors, providing taxpayer services, obtaining work permits and visas, securing social security, acquiring land and property, obtaining sectoral permits and establishing export processing zones (https://eregulations.invest.go.ke/). To secure a business permit, the government has instituted reforms that have decreased the number of procedures and days required to secure such permits. For example, the county government of Nairobi launched an Online QR code that provides a unique identification for all approved architectural and structural plans (EOD, p. 38), making it easy for commercial and individual real estate developers to quickly secure the required permits to begin work.

11 Financial Services – There are over 40 financial institutions in Kenya, and these institutions are licensed and regulated by the Central Bank of Kenya. For example, Equity Bank Holdings was founded in 1984 and is Kenya's youngest bank, yet, today, it is Kenya's largest multinational company. In 2022, Equity Group was ranked the fifth strongest banking brand worldwide. Standard Chartered Bank is the oldest of all banks in Kenya since it was established in 1911 (Equity Group Website). Other banks in Kenya include Kenya Commercial Bank, Cooperative Bank of Kenya and National Bank of Kenya, Stanbic Bank, and Commercial Bank of Kenya. For additional information on top banks in Kenya, the reader is referred to an article published by CFI (Top Banks in Kenya). The Kenya Bankers Association is the financial sector's leading advocacy group (https://www.kba.co.ke/index.php).

12 Savings and Credit Cooperative Organizations (SACCOs) – In addition to regular financial institutions, as noted in Chapter 3, Kenyans also have

the option of investing their money in SACCOs. SACCOs are formed when individuals with similar interests register a credit union with the Ministry of Cooperatives. Once the SACCO is registered it can take deposits and issue low-interest loans. SACCOs have played a dominant role in the economy by spearheading savings and investments in Kenya. SACCOs are regulated, licensed and supervised by the SACCO Societies Regulatory Authority (SASRA). Some of the most important SACCOs are Stima Sacco, Safaricom Sacco, Kenya Police Sacco, Kenya USA Diaspora Sacco, Mhasibu Sacco, etc. (Musili, 2022) or read Stephen Murithi's (2020) article on the best SACCOs to join.

13 Mobile Financial Services – As highlighted in Chapter 5, mobile financial services are vibrant in Kenya. For example, M-PESA (PESA means the money in Swahili), a Vodafone Safaricom product, introduced mobile money to Kenyans in 2007. M-PESA enables a user to receive money via a text message without having a traditional bank account. M-PESA completely changed the lives of Kenyans, particularly the unbanked. Today, Kenya has one of the highest mobile money penetration in the world, and one can pay for everything using M-PESA. The authors have utilized M-PESA services for riding taxis, purchasing vegetables from street vendors, purchasing airline tickets, etc. According to the Communications Authority of Kenya, in September 2021, M-PESA had 98 percent of registered mobile money customers, while Airtel Money and Telkom's T-Kash shared the remaining 1.6 percent. Moreover, 96 percent of all households in Kenya have at least one person who can make transactions on M-PESA. M-PESA is a dominant payment platform in Kenya. In February 2022, the Central Bank of Kenya unveiled a new payment strategy for 2022–2025 (Central Bank, 2022). In this strategy, the CBK will evaluate the national payment ecosystem to facilitate competition to offer consumers more choices.

14 Insurance – There are 49 registered insurance companies in Kenya. The Kenya Insurance Regulatory Authority (IRA), was established by an Amendment to the Insurance Act in 2006. The mandate of the IRA is to regulate, supervise, and develop the insurance industry.

15 According to the Association of Kenyan Insurers' (2019) report, non-life insurance businesses account for 56.93 percent of the industry's gross premium income, with motor and medical insurance accounting for 69.14 percent of the non–life gross premium. In 2020, IRA had registered 24 life insurance companies and three reinsurers. The main products in Kenya are ordinary life, group life, and pensions. Group credit, annuities, and investment continue to grow but at a slower rate. Figure 7.2 shown below, was developed by IRA and analyzed by Deloitte (2020) and provides additional information on the key players in the industry (Figure 7.3).

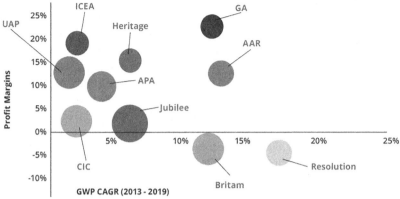

Figure 7.2 Top Ten General Insurance Players Performance 2013–2019.

Source: IRA Kenya Industry Reports 2013–2019.

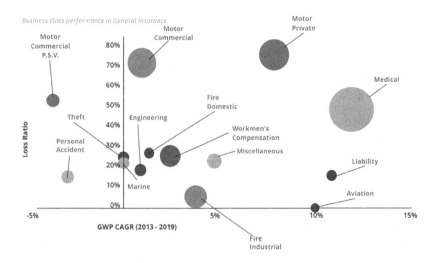

Figure 7.3 Business Class Performance in General Insurance.

Source: IRA Kenya Industry Reports 2013–2019.

7.4 Basic Infrastructure and Supply Chain Management

7.4.1 Transportation

The Kenyan government has a highly developed infrastructure compared to other countries in the region. Kenya has four international airports (located in Nairobi, Mombasa, Eldoret, and Kisumu) and several domestic airports, aerodromes, and airstrips. Nairobi is the transportation hub for east and central Africa. The port of Mombasa is one of the most important ports in the region as it supplies the needs of several of Kenya's landlocked neighbors. The Mombasa port is an important logistics hub for the region. It is the largest port in East Africa and the second largest in Africa. The Standard Gauge Railway (SGR) is a railway that connects Nairobi and Mombasa. The SGR has provided passenger as well as freight rail services since 2017. The government continues to invest in railways, and the Nairobi Naivasha railway was completed in 2019.

In addition, the government has invested heavily in road infrastructure. Currently, of the 177,800 kilometers of classified and unclassified roads, approximately 16,902 are paved (Masyuko U.S. Embassy Nairobi, 2021). Under Vision 2030, the government has earmarked over 5,000 kilometers of roads for improvements, and some projects have been completed. For example, the Thika Superhighway eased traffic in Central Kenya. At the same time, the new Nairobi expressway is expected to ease traffic by connecting Mlolongo in Machakos to Jomo Kenyatta International Airport to the Nairobi-Nakuru highway (Daley, 2021). This expressway is important since it is part of the northern corridor that provides passage to 85 percent of cargo headed to the Democratic Republic of Congo, Rwanda, South Sudan. Kenya is also part of the LAPSSET Highway, an inter-regional highway linking Kenya, South Sudan, and Addis Ababa. For additional information on current roads under construction in Kenya, see Roberto Muyelo's 2020 article on Tuko.

7.4.2 Information and Communications Technology (ICT)

Kenya's technological infrastructure is adequately developed. It is the regional leader in terms of general ICT infrastructure, value-added services, mobile money, and mobile banking services (US embassy Kenya, Country Commercial Guide). In Sub-Saharan Africa, Kenya ranked fourth as one of the fastest-growing e-commerce economies according to the 2020 UNCTAD B2C Commerce Index (Kenya Commercial Guide E-commerce). Additionally, 72.9 percent of Kenyans use a mobile money account, and 26.1 percent make purchases and pay bills online (according to the World Bank Financial Inclusion Data). 59.24 million mobile connections, 11.0 million social media users, and 21.75 million internet users represent 40 percent penetration (Digital 2021: Kenya). The four major providers are Safaricom at 71.2 percent market share, Airtel at 17.6 percent, Telkom Kenya at 7.4 percent and Finserve Africa/Equitel at 3.8 percent. The government continues to invest in ICT and in FY 2021/2022, provided $210 million for ICT initiatives. These initiatives include, among others, Konza Technopolis, which is planned as a world-class city that will be powered by a thriving ICT sector with a superior infrastructure and business-friendly governance systems. This project, located in Machakos (about 70 miles from Nairobi), is part of Kenya's Vision 2030 economic development portfolio (Vision 2030.go.ke/. Other projects include investment in a Digital Literacy Program (DLP) and the maintenance and installation of Fiber Optic Cables.

7.4.3 Energy

The Kenyan government continues to invest in the energy sector, focusing on last-mile connections to small businesses and households. There are now more than 7.8 million customers who have electricity connections. In 2019, Kenya was ranked 40th in the Renewable Energy Country Attractiveness Index by Ernst & Young (E&Y ranking). In 2019, the World Bank, the World Health Organization, and the International Energy Agency ranked Kenya as one of the countries with improved electricity access by the widest margins. BloombergNEF (BNEF) ranked Kenya in the top 5 in global energy rankings. In 2019, Kenya was ranked 70 globally, while in Sub-Saharan Africa, Kenya was ranked third. To ensure consistent electricity for businesses, in 2021, the government enacted the Energy Reliability, Quality of Supply, and Service on Electricity Supply Outages Regulations. These regulations introduced a penalty imposed by the Energy and Petroleum Regulatory Authority (EPRA) on any registered energy supplier that exceeds the limit of capped power outages. This will address persistent power outages that companies and individuals continue to face from their service providers. As noted in Chapter 2, the energy sector in Kenya continues to grow with continued investments in renewable energy. For example, the Lake Turkana Wind Power Project (LTWP) is a farm that is valued at over $823 million, and it can supply power to more than one million homes. Another important project is the Akiira Geothermal Project, a landmark power project in the East African power sector with plans to develop a 70 Megawatts geothermal power plant. The project, a privately financed and independent venture, is a greenfield geothermal power plant that extends Kenya's innovation in the geothermal power plant (http://akiiraone.com/about-us/).

7.4.4 Supply Chain Management

Kenya is an East African region's leading logistics and trade hub (Karani, 2021). As discussed earlier, the government continues to invest in projects that will further enhance the infrastructure. The Kenya Institute of Supplies Management (KISM) is a public entity established under the "Supplies Practitioners Management Act No. 17 of 2007 to "promote learning, development of best practices, and application of the same to the practice of procurement and supply chain management" (KISM website). KISM licenses and regulates the procurement and supply chain management

(P&SCM) profession in Kenya (KISM Strategic Plan, 2020–2024). All procurement and supply chain management practitioners in Kenya must be registered by KISM and pay the subscription fees and annual dues.

7.5 Corporate Social Responsibility (CSR)

Corporate social responsibility was briefly discussed in Chapter 6. Most CSR projects in Kenya are centered around education, economic empowerment, health, water, sports and cultural engagements, and environmental conservation, among many others. Companies are expected to engage in CSR projects, and any business organization operating in Kenya can select from many CSR projects. In Chapter 6, there was a discussion of gender inequality in Kenya. To this end, many organizations work primarily with women's groups to close the gender gap. Therefore, companies have many opportunities to participate in CSR activities centered on gender equality.

7.6 Conclusion

This chapter has presented the benefits of starting a business in Kenya. Corruption and other related problems were identified as impediments to a successful business. Nonetheless, the chapter has outlined the benefits of starting a business in Kenya. In addition, the chapter demonstrates that the infrastructure, human capital, and facilitating organizations are poised and ready to support any new business in Kenya.

References

Akiira Geothermal, http://akiiraone.com/about-us/), retrieved April 28, 2022.

Association of Kenyan Insurance Industry Report (2020). https://www.akinsure.com/content/uploads/documents/AKI_Insurance_Industry_Report_2020.pdf, retrieved May 20, 2022.

Central Bank (2022). https://www.centralbank.go.ke/wp-content/uploads/2022/02/National-Payments-Strategy-2022-2025.pdf, retrieved May 20, 2022.

Cia Factbook, https://www.cia.gov/the-world-factbook/countries/kenya/, retrieved March 2, 2022, retrieved, May 20, 2022.

Daley, B. (2021). Nairobis-new-expressway-may-ease-traffic-woes-but-mostly-for-the-wealthy," https://theconversation.com/nairobis-new-expressway-may-ease-traffic-woes-but-mostly-for-the-wealthy-170164, retrieved March 1, 2022.

Deca, K. (2020). "Why Kenya tops Africa's business destination of choice," (https://afrikanheroes.com/2020/01/30/why-kenya-tops-africas-business-destination-of-choice/ retrieved, May 20, 2022.

DBRT, https://brs.go.ke/assets/downloads/Kenya-Business-Climate-Reforms-Milestone-Report-2020-2021.pdf, retrieved, May 20, 2022.

Deloitte, Insurance outlook report 2020/21 East Africa November 2020, https://www2.deloitte.com/content/dam/Deloitte/ke/Documents/financial-services/Insurance%20Outlook%20Report%20EA%202020.pdf, retrieved May 15 2022.

Digital Kenya (2021). https://datareportal.com/reports/digital-2021-kenya), retrieved May 20, 2022.

e-Citizen website. https://www.ecitizen.go.ke/ecitizen-services.html, retrieved April 28, 2022.

Ecofin Agency (2019). https://www.ecofinagency.com/public-management/0301-39479-forbes-unveils-its-ranking-of-best-countries-for-business-in-2019-here-are-the-african-best, retrieved May 15 2022.

Ernst and Young (E&Y ranking). https://assets.ey.com/content/dam/ey-sites/ey-com/en_gl/topics/power-and-utilities/ey-recai-58th-edition-top-40-ranking-october-2021.pdf, retrieved May 20, 2022.

Export.gov, Kenya Commercial Guide. https://www.trade.gov/country-commercial-guides/kenya-investment-climate-statement), retrieved May 20, 2022.

Equity Group Website, Equity Group Ranked the 5th Strongest Banking Brand in the World (2022). https://equitygroupholdings.com/equity-group-ranked-the-5th-strongest-banking-brand-in-the-world/, retrieved February 28, 2022.

Federation of Kenya Employers (FKE). https://www.fke-kenya.org/ retrieved May 25 2022.

Karani, J. (2021). Why Kenya's supply chain is ahead in the region, https://www.standardmedia.co.ke/opinion/article/2001428405/why-kenyas-supply-chain-is-ahead-in-the-region, November 7, 2021, retrieved February 2, 2022.

Kenya Association of Manufacturers (KAM). https://kam.co.ke/. retrieved May 15 2022.

Kenya Bankers Association (KBA). https://www.kba.co.ke/index.php retrieved May 15 2022.

Kenya-Country Commercial Guide, E-commerce. https://www.trade.gov/country-commercial-guides/kenya-ecommerce, retrieved May 20, 2022.

Kenya Institute of Supplies Management (KISM Website). https://kism.or.ke/ retrieved April 28, 2022.

Kenya Insurance Regulatory Authority (IRA). https://www.ira.go.ke/ retrieved May 15 2022.

Kenya Investment Authority (KenInvest). https://eregulations.invest.go.ke/ retrieved May 15 2022.

Kenya Investment Authority (KenInvest). http://www.invest.go.ke/who-we-are/ retrieved May 15 2022.

Kenya National Chamber of Commerce and Industry (KNCCI). https://www.kenyachamber.or.ke/about-kncci/ retrieved May 15 2022.

Kenya Private Sector Alliance (KEPSA). https://kepsa.or.ke/. retrieved May 15 2022.

Kenya Revenue Authority (KRA). https://www.kra.go.ke/en/about-kra retrieved May 15 2022).

Kenya Youth Unemployment Rate. (1991-2022). https://www.macrotrends.net/countries/KEN/kenya/youth-unemployment-rate retrieved May 15 2022.

Konza Technopolis. https://konza.go.ke/, retrieved May 2, 2022.

Masyuko, M. (2021). Design and construction, country commercial guide https://www.trade.gov/country-commercial-guides/kenya-design-and-construction, 2021-09-13, retrieved February 28, 2022.

Murithi, S. (2020). Best Saccos to join in Kenya, September 2, 2020. https://www.qazini.com/best-saccos-to-join-in-kenya/. retrieved May 20, 2022.

Musili, M. (2022). 15 best Saccos in Kenya for savings and investment in 2022, https://www.tuko.co.ke/259866-15-saccos-kenya-savings-investment.html retrieved May 15 2022.

Muyela, R. (2020). Key road projects across Kenya that are shaping Uhuru Kenyatta's legacy, https://www.tuko.co.ke/382395-key-road-projects-kenya-shaping-uhuru-kenyattas-legacy.html, retrieved February 28, 2022.

Nailab Website, Sam Gichuru. https://nailab.co/about%20us, retrieved March 7, 2022.

National Environment Management Authority (NEMA). https://www.nema.go.ke/ retrieved May 15 2022.

National Social Security Fund (NSSF). https://www.nssf.or.ke/ retrieved May 15 2022.

National Hospital Insurance Fund (NHIF). http://www.nhif.or.ke/healthinsurance/ retrieved May 15 2022.

Nyoike, V. (2021). Best business incubators in Kenya for entrepreneurs. https://businessideas4africa.com/incubators-kenya retrieved October 15 2022.

Strategic Plan (2020-2024). The center of excellence for supply chain management practitioners competent and ethical supply chain management practitioners https://kism.or.ke/wp-content/uploads/2021/11/KISM-Strategic-Plan-Abridged-Version.pdf, retrieved February 28, 2022.

Thembekwayo, V. (2016). What SA entrepreneurs can learn from Kenyans https://vusithembekwayo.com/what-sa-entrepreneurs-can-learn-from-kenyans/ retrieved March 7, 2022.

Top Banks in Kenya. https://corporatefinanceinstitute.com/resources/careers/companies/top-banks-in-kenya/, retrieved May 2, 2022.

Transparency International. (https://www.statista.com/statistics/1286269/corruption-perception-index-in-kenya/). retrieved March 7, 2022.

Vision 2030. https://vision2030.go.ke/). retrieved April 28, 2022.

World Bank. Doing Business 2020, economic profile Kenya, https://www.doingbusiness.org/content/dam/doingBusiness/country/k/kenya/KEN.pdf, retrieved February 28, 2022.

8 The Marketing Process

8.1 Introduction

Marketing is all about exchange, and wherever one goes in the world, the process of exchange among all kinds of cultures, political structures, or economic arrangements is observed. "Marketing is the activity, set of institutions, and processes for creating, communicating, delivering and exchanging offerings that have value for customers, clients, partners and society at large (American Marketing Association AMA, 2017). The marketing concept states that an organization should strive to satisfy the needs of their customers while also achieving organizational goals. There are many definitions of the marketing concept. Still, an early definition was offered by McNamara (1972, p. 51) "(the) marketing concept is a philosophy of business management, based upon a company-wide acceptance of the need for customer orientation, profit orientation, and recognition of the important role of marketing in communicating the needs of the market to all major corporate departments."

The generally accepted means of implementing the marketing concept is the marketing mix model (or the 4Ps of marketing, i.e. product, place, price, and promotion). Professor E. Jerome McCarthy first used the 4P's shorthand reference in 1960. The manipulation of the marketing mix variables for a specific target market enables a company to develop marketing strategies focused on customer needs and wants. The product, tangible or intangible, begins the marketing process. The price is what the customer gives up in exchange for the product or the service. For companies, price represents revenue and profits. Promotion refers to how the company will communicate product offerings to its target market. At its most basic level, place refers to where a customer can buy the product or access the service.

An effective marketing mix results in a value proposition that customers can clearly understand. Marketing environments are everchanging. Therefore, businesses must develop a market orientation. Kohli and Jaworski (1990, p. 3) defined market orientation as "the organization-wide generation of market intelligence, dissemination of the intelligence across departments and organization-wide responsiveness to it." The marketing field is divided

DOI: 10.4324/9781003095156-8

into many sub-functions, such as personal selling, advertising, marketing communication, distribution, market research, and consumer behavior, among many others. The different marketing activities work in tandem to ensure that a firm is satisfying customer needs while simultaneously building long-term relationships with its customers and meeting organizational objectives. In today's environment, many firms engage in cross-national business. Therefore, we turn our attention to international marketing.

8.2 International Marketing

International marketing has been defined as "the performance of business activities designed to plan, price, promote, and direct the flow of a company's goods and services to consumers or users in more than one nation for a profit" (Cateora et al., 2020, p. 10). Hence, international marketing differs from domestic marketing because it involves a firm making one or more marketing decisions across national borders. Sometimes, a firm may establish manufacturing and marketing facilities overseas, which calls for coordinating marketing strategies across markets. Undoubtedly, an international company operating in several countries will deal with different uncontrollable forces in each market. Moreover, controllable factors such as cost and price structures, opportunities for advertising, and distribution infrastructure are also likely to differ significantly in different national markets (Business Fundamentals, 2011).

8.3 Marketing Environment in Kenya

Over the last decade, the Internet has become an important marketing channel, allowing customers and firms to participate in domestic and international business transactions (Lim et al., 2016). As a result, selling goods and services via the Internet, or online retailing has become incredibly user-friendly and powerful. (Mathew & Mishra, 2014). E-commerce experts across the globe have made it easy, fast and convenient for consumers to shop for apparel, cosmetics, groceries and other consumer products online (Paul 2019). Shopping online in Kenya is a growing source of growth for retail firms. The Internet has dramatically revised the methods retailers use to display, advertise, sell and correspond with customers. The Internet in Kenya provides a global marketplace that extends beyond the traditional geographic markets where consumers generally shop. Online shopping has triggered a shopping revolution that is restructuring the local retailing environment, making it an investment choice for retailing entrepreneurs (Mang'era et al., 2019). Kenya has a youthful population who are internet savvy and are increasingly comfortable with digital transactions, particularly due to the ease of payment using mobile payments such as M-PESA. A recent study by Mastercard on consumer spending showed that four out of five consumers in Kenya had shopped online for data, apparel, healthcare, banking and other fast-moving consumer goods (Mastercard Press Release, 2021. In Kenya, one of the challenges of online retailing has been delays in delivery times due to infrastructure issues such as bad roads, traffic jams, etc. Some e-commerce platforms, such as Jumia, and others use motorcycles (Bodabodas) for quick and fast delivery. Uber and Bolt have also become trusted delivery options. The photos below show Naivas supermarket promoting bodaboda delivery (Figure 8.1).

8.4 The Marketing Mix in Kenya

8.4.1 Price

Product prices vary depending on the product category, availability of alternatives, and supply and demand. Generally, Kenyans are price sensitive and may often compromise on quality if there are cheaper alternatives

Figure 8.1 Billboard Advertisement Naivas Supermarket.

Source: Photo by author.

(Country Commercial Guide, 2021). There are cheaper alternatives from suppliers in China and India for most product categories. Nonetheless, consumers value international brands and the rising middle class can afford and is willing to pay higher prices for quality. For most product categories, a consumer can buy a "local" or international brand (usually referred to as "imported"). Another factor for consideration is the "kadogo" economy; kadogo, which means "small", is well established in Kenya (Mbego, 2019). The kadogo economy enables consumers to make small daily purchases of needed items such as milk, bread, cigarettes, cooking oil, kerosene, etc. Therefore, many leading brands offer smaller lower-priced versions of their products to cater to the kadogo economy.

Service companies like Safaricom and Airtel offer phone credit in small denominations to cater for the kadogo economy. Consumer packaged companies also sell small-sized packages of their products. For example, Unilever sells its Omo hand washing powder in 500 grams up to 3.5-kilogram sizes. The kadogo economy also is evident in other regions of the world, such as India. According to Interbrand India, many brands developed products at the (five) rupees level (referred to as the "magic five") formula to drive consumer trials, engage consumers, and demolish basic entry-level barriers (Bhushan and Pande (2010). Prices in Kenya are regulated by the Competition Authority of Kenya (Competition Authority of Kenya, 2022).

Some products and services may also be subject to Value Added Tax (VAT). For additional information on VAT, the reader is encouraged to visit the Kenya Revenue Authority (KRA) website for current VAT rates and other pertinent information.

8.4.2 Product

Products sold in Kenya must be adapted to suit the needs and tastes of the Kenyan consumer. Since products are quite varied, this section provides general information about products sold in the Kenyan market. All imported products must be labeled in English and/or Kiswahili. Here is an example of cigarettes that demonstrate the use of both languages in Kenya (Figure 8.2 and 8.3).

All imported products must be cleared using the services of a clearing agent. Additionally, Kenya has a pre-shipment requirement for export destined to Kenya. In some cases, an import license is required, particularly for health, security or environmental products. Many online resources can provide timely information to an importer to Kenya. The Kenya Bureau of Standards (KEBS) is the primary government agency responsible for developing standards and quality control. The agency offers several marks of quality. The fortification logo is issued when a company demonstrates that a food has been fortified with more vitamins or minerals. Standardization is a mandatory product certification scheme for all locally manufactured goods. The diamond mark of quality is awarded to local and international manufacturers who have

Figure 8.2 Product Example with English and Kiswahili Languages – English.
Source: Photos by author.

demonstrated a high degree of excellence in manufacturing and quality. The import standardization marks/stickers were developed in 2015 to deal with fake KEBS quality marks and to give consumers the ability to authenticate the marks before purchasing goods. Additional information on the KEBS marks can be found on the KEBS website.

8.4.3 Place

There are multiple ways for companies to sell their products in Kenya: traditional supermarkets, grocery stores; malls, kiosks; small shops; street vendors; and many informal sector merchants. Carrefour, Chandarana, Quickmart, EastMatt, and Naivas are some of the largest supermarkets in Kenya. Many malls such as Two Rivers Mall, The Junction Mall, Westgate

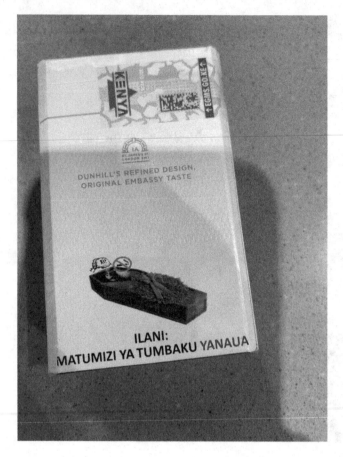

Figure 8.3 Product Example with English and Kiswahili Languages – Kiswahili.
Source: Photos by author.

Shopping Mall, The Waterfront Karen, Garden City Mall, TRM -Thika Road Mall, The Hub Karen, Capital Centre, Galleria Mall, Yaya Centre, Lavington Mall, Sarit Centre, among many others, are found in the environs of Nairobi. There are shopping centers that are easily accessible to consumers in most major cities and towns, and much local mom-and-pop shops, as well as small kiosks where consumers can make purchases, cab be fiybd as well. A 2019 study by Nielsen found that traditional trade (kiosks and groceries) accounted for 66.3 percent of retail sector transactions, while modern trade (supermarkets) accounted for 33.7 percent (Mbego, 2019). Many street vendors/hawkers who sell products as diverse as oranges, belts, artwork, sunglasses, etc., can be found everywhere in Kenyan cities and towns. In their recent article, Kimani et al. (2020, p. 159) acknowledged hawking, particularly in Nairobi. They stated: "hawking as a practice in

Nairobi central business district streets, and hawkers as the actors is as old as the city itself … and hawking is bound to remain a feature of the urban landscape". In addition to various hawkers, some vendors sell products using pushcarts. Examples of products sold on pushcarts include "Farmers Choice Sausages" and ice-cream, etc. pineapples, and many fruits are also sold from "mkokotenis". A mkokoteni is a small cart that is open and has wheels. Mkototenis are also used for the transportation of products, particularly fresh products, from farmers' markets to desired destinations. The Kenya National Alliance of Street Vendors and Informal Traders (KEN-ASVIT) is an umbrella organization that brings together street vendors, hawkers, and informal traders in twelve of Kenya's major towns.

Finally, Kenya is one of the key logistical conduits into the East African Community (EAC), and many foreign companies have established their regional headquarters in Kenya (U.S. Commerce Service, 2012). Many considerations come into play when negotiating an agent or distributor agreement with a potential Kenyan partner. Specific factors influence the degree of vertical integration in the channels in the marketing environment. Hence, a better understanding of the current marketing structures in Kenya and other African countries can help to predict structural changes that will ensue from any anticipated changes in the marketing environment (Dijkstra et al., 2001).

8.4.4 Promotion in Kenya

A company doing business in Kenya will find that many marketing agencies are offering traditional and digital marketing services. For a partial listing of marketing agencies in Kenya, see www.Soravjain.com. The Media Council of Kenya is the media regulator in Kenya, while the Kenya Film Classification Board is the regulator of films. This section will cover the traditional promotional mix, emphasizing how some of the traditional forms of promotion differ in Kenya as opposed to other regions of the world. For example, we highlight the importance of radio advertising in Kenya and the proliferation of billboards and unipoles.

8.4.4.1 Advertising

A company doing business in Kenya has many options when it comes to advertising. It can choose from billboard, radio, television (TV), social media advertising, etc. We will discuss each of these options below. Many international advertising agencies such as Ogilvy & Mather, McCann Erickson, Publicis and Omnicom, and Young and Rubicam have offices in Kenya. These international agencies often work with local advertising agencies to adapt advertising for Kenyan customers. Top Image Africa (TIA) is one of the local agencies that works with many local and international brands. In an interview with one of the authors at their Nairobi offices, **Jennifer Barassa founder of TIA noted that her business philosophy is,** "*to perform superbly always, surpassing the clients' expectations*", **(Barassa, 2022) TIA is a below-the-line advertising entity, whose promotion strategy is** "*taking the product directly to the consumer*" **through customer engagement, merchandising, promotions and billboard advertising.**

8.4.4.2 Billboard Advertising and Unipoles

The use of billboards to advertise products is very important in Kenya. When driving or walking in most cities and towns in Kenya, one can see a preponderance of billboards. In bigger cities such as Nairobi, the billboards line major streets, particularly at intersections. Many companies offer billboard advertising, and Alliance Media Kenya is one of the largest home media agencies. It offers outdoor advertising, billboard advertising, digital billboards, airport advertising, shopping mall advertising, and street pole advertising across the country. According to their website, Alliance Media has been voted as the best billboard company in Kenya and has been awarded superbrand status in East Africa for many years. Billboard advertising has transformed the landscape of most towns in Kenya. Below are examples of billboards on Ngong Road in Nairobi, which were photographed by one of the authors in December 2021. Unipoles are extensively used in Kenya since they are visible from afar and can easily withstand wind and temperature variations. Ironically, the unipoles found in neighborhoods take away their serenity and beauty (Figures 8.4–8.7).

Truck advertising is also very common in Kenya. An example from Aquamist was co-promoting their mineral water with their Fruitz (Guava, Apple, and tropical) fruit juices. The photo of the truck was captured in December 2021 in front of Maguna Sagana supermarket, where the truck was parked. A DJ was playing music to attract shoppers to the truck and the brand (Figure 8.8).

Another form of outdoor advertising is the painting of buildings. This is a very effective way of advertising that is not only found in Kenya but also other regions of the world. It is noteworthy that some brands like Safaricom, Coca-Cola, and DSTV have transformed the landscape, particularly in rural areas where you cannot miss the brands in the middle of a green landscape. See pictures taken in January 2022 by one of the authors (Figures 8.9 and 8.10).

8.4.4.3 Radio Advertising

Radio Advertising continues to be prevalent and effective, particularly since radio ads can quickly reach desired target audiences. Over 100 private and non-profit regional radio stations broadcast in many different languages. Often radio ads need to be translated into the primary language of a specific

Figure 8.4 Unipoles Advertising – Galitos.

Source: Photo by author.

target market. English language and Swahili language radio stations have a large listening audience. KBC, Citizen FM, Kiss FM, and Classic FM are some of the most popular Kenyan radio stations. Some popular local language channels include Kameme FM, Inoro FM (both Kikuyu radio stations); Chamgei FM, Kass FM (both Kalenjin), Lake Victoria (Luo),

Figure 8.5 Unipole Advertising – Amaize.

Source: Photo by author.

Mulembe FM (Luhya) Mbaitu FM (Kamba), Star FM (Somali) Egesa FM (Kisii) and Metro East FM (Hindi). Some radio talk show hosts have large listening audiences and serve as brand ambassadors and influencers. Maina Kageni is a popular morning talk radio host (Classic 105) with a large

Figure 8.6 Unipole Advertising – Tuzo Milk.

Source: Photo by author.

listening audience for his early morning show. Radio remains an important promotional medium in Kenya, and radio advertising revenue in Kenya is projected to reach US dollar 128 million by 2023 (Statistica, 2022). The figure below shows the upward trend of radio advertising in Kenya (Figure 8.11).

Figure 8.7 Unipole Advertising – Tusker Malt.
Source: Photo by author.

8.4.4.4 TV Advertising

There are several large-scale privately-owned media companies as well as government-owned state media. Kenya Broadcasting Corporation is a state-owned corporation that broadcasts in English and Swahili, as well as several

Figure 8.8 Truck Advertising – Aquamist – Fruitz.

Source: Photo by author.

Figure 8.9 DSTV Painted Building.

Source: Photo by author.

Figure 8.10 Del Monte Painted Building.
Source: Photo by author.

local languages. One of the largest private media houses is Royal Media Services, which operates three TV stations and fourteen radio stations. When Kenya moved from analog broadcasting systems to digital platforms, the number of television stations in the country increased significantly. Popular TV stations include Citizen TV, NTV, K24, KBC, KTN, and many others. Companies doing business in Kenya can advertise on various TV stations broadcasting in English, Kiswahili, or local languages. TV stations have individual rate cards, which are easily obtainable from the online portals of most media companies. Furthermore, many advertising agencies offer promotional services, including TV advertising. For a quick introduction to different media options in Kenya, the reader can consult online resources such as those provided by the Empire Group.

8.4.4.5 Newspaper Advertising

The Standard Newspapers and The Daily Nation are Kenya's national daily newspapers. The Daily Nation is the region's most widely read newspaper, while the Standard is the oldest\and has a significant market share. The East African primarily covers stories from the East African region, including some international stories. Taifa Leo is a Swahili-language newspaper that is published daily. Business Daily is a daily publication that covers business

Radio advertising revenue in Kenya from 2013 to 2023

(in million U.S. dollars)

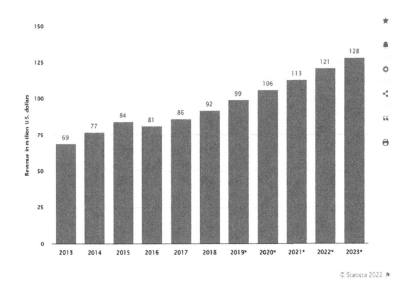

Figure 8.11 Radio Advertising Revenue.

news and extensively analyzes business topics. The advertising rate cards for the newspapers are easily obtainable from their websites. The Daily Nation rate card is available at https://www.mwnation.com/rate-card/. The Nation Publications Limited (NPL) rate card delineates advertising rates for local, government, and international entities.

8.4.4.6 Social Media Advertising

Social media advertising has become increasingly important in Kenya. Internet penetration in Kenya is around eighty-five percent, with over twenty-two million active users (UNESCO, 2021). It is noteworthy that internet usage among Kenyan youth is even higher and is mainly used for social media (UNESCO, 2021). This high internet penetration undoubtedly makes it possible for companies to deploy various social media advertising tools. A company can utilize Facebook, Whatsapp, Instagram, TikTok, YouTube, mobile phones, and advertising on company websites to reach Kenyan consumers. A world population review ranking shows over 10 million Facebook users in Kenya (World Population Review, 2021). In 2021, Ajua revealed that Kenya had the highest percentage of monthly WhatsApp users compared to the rest of the world. Kenya leads the world in Whatsapp usage, as over 97 percent of internet users in Kenya use Whatsapp every month. Whatsapp has become the platform for many small businesses in Africa (Otieno, 2021). Instagram usage is also very high in Kenya and some celebrities, such as Eunice Wanjiru Njoki, aka mammitoeunice, a Kenyan comedian, have over one million Instagram followers (Figure 8.12).

8.4.4.7 Social Media Influencers: Brand Ambassadors

There are many social media influencers, and the range and variety of these influencers have continued to increase; the Covid-19 pandemic created even more of them. During the pandemic, Tik Tok became the most globally downloaded app globally. Elsa Majimbo, a Kenyan comedian and social media influencer, gained fame in early 2021 for her monologues in which she was crunching on potato chips. Elsa gained fame in Kenya and also garnered international fame. The Italian brand Valentino collaborated with Elsa, and she became the brand ambassador for MAC cosmetics and Rihanna's Fenty glasses. Another social media influencer is Felix Odour (aka Jalango). In 2021, Jalango stated that he was a brand ambassador for five top brands (such as Mwananchi credit) and an influencer of 1001 brands (Boyo, 2021). Other key brand ambassadors include Janet Mbugua (Lifebuoy); Sauti Sol (Chrome Vodka); Size 8 (Softcare Diapers); Anita Nderu (Uber Kenya); Maina Kageni and Adell Onyango (Johnnie Walker); Esther Akoth (aka Akothee, Rosy brand) and Shiru wa GP (Optiven Group). Other famous influencers include Eric Omondi (comedian), Betty Kyalo (media personality); Robert Alai (blogger), Churchill (comedy

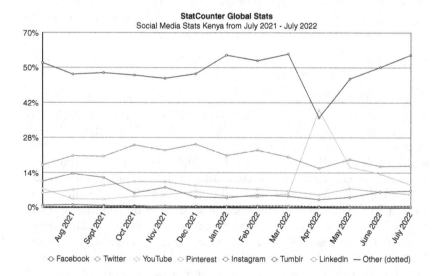

Figure 8.12 Social Media StatCounter.

business) Jeff Koinange (news anchor), Maxine Wabosha (YouTuber), among many others (Gitonga, 2020). While the social medial influencers highlighted are not exhaustive, they clearly show that a company can garner a lot of views by utilizing some of them.

8.4.4.8 YouTube Advertising and Sponsorship

Another avenue for marketing a product is the sponsorship of YouTube shows, particularly talk shows. Using celebrity endorsers has always been a powerful way for brands to market their products. This is because celebrity endorsers can easily maintain attention and high recall rates for messages due to their fame and connection to their fan base (Croft et al., 1996). In his review of celebrity endorsement research, Erdogan (1999, p. 292) noted, "celebrities have been endorsing products since the late nineteenth century." So, while YouTube shows represent a different medium for using celebrity endorsers, the method of influence remains the same as what has happened in the past. Because of the proliferation of YouTube channels and talk shows in Kenya, we will highlight only two of them, both done in English and Kiswahili. The first talk show is the Lynn Ngugi show. In 2022, Lynn Ngugi won best digital content creator at the women in film awards.

Some highly ranked YouTube talk shows are filmed at a hotel in Kenya. At the show's beginning, hosts usually thank the hotel for providing the shooting location. Consequently, Lynn begins her show by thanking West Wood Hotel for providing the shooting location. Additionally, her show prominently displays the logo of Optiven Group (a real estate company), and Lynn always thanks "Elegant Fashions Kenya" for providing the wardrobe for the episode that is being recorded. These types of sponsorships and verbal endorsements are excellent promotional methods for these brands. Jalango has perfected the brand endorsement on his Jalango TV show; he prominently displays the "Velvex – hand sanitizer" on the coffee table and sanitizes the hands of every guest using Velvex at the beginning of every show. The Jalango show is filmed at the Mialle Restaurant, and Jalango promotes the restaurant by ordering food for his guests at the show's end. Brands such as Mwananchi Credit Loans, Shell, and others provide the show's framing.

YouTube will continue to be an important area for brands to advertise in. In 2021, YouTube released a statement stating that "Kenyan YouTube content creators would now be paid up to KSh1.1 million every month for short 15-second videos uploaded as a bonus payment" (Business Daily, 2021). This will motivate more content creators to enter this creative space since Kenyans were previously only paid for videos and music that were longer. Some music videos garner a lot of views; for example, in 2021, Shiru wa GP (Kikuyu gospel artist) became the first female gospel musician in Kenya to garner over 69 million views.

8.4.4.9 Sponsorship

Companies doing business have the option of sponsoring many different events. Many sponsorship programs center around health, education, and the environment. Also, many companies sponsor sporting events. In 2022, Safaricom announced sponsorship of KShs.20 million of the Magical Kenya Ladies Open Golf Tournament, which is part of the Ladies European Golf Tour held in Kilifi (KBC, 2022). ABSA Financial Group also sponsored the Magical Kenya Open Golf tournament with a KShs.56 million sponsorship (Ngala, Daily Nation, 2022). Company sponsorship of sporting events is still a very popular way of promoting a brand or a company. In Kenya, a company can choose to sponsor athletics, football (soccer), rugby, and swimming, among many sports.

Soccer remains one of the most popular sports in Kenya, and Kenyan marathon runners are ranked the best in the world. In March 2022, the Ministry of Sports, Culture, and Heritage, through a letter by the Cabinet Secretary for Sports Amina Mohamed, clarified the guidelines for sponsors. The letter stated: "Any person sponsoring sports activities must seek prior approval from the Cabinet Secretary responsible for sports on the amount he intends to spend to sponsor sports". Moreover, the Ministry encouraged all sponsors and partners to ensure that most of the sponsorship monies were athlete-centered (Mutuiri, 2022). The Kenyan government offers tax rebates by exempting individuals or companies from paying taxes on any money spent sponsoring sports (Otieno, Daily Nation 2022). Companies in Kenya usually sponsor sports teams, and these teams are often named after the company or its dominant brands. A recent article on March 11, 2022, Daily Nation newspaper, illustrates the brand reinforcement power of these types of sponsorships through the naming conventions of the teams (Otieno, 2022). The Football Kenya Federation Premier League champions are known as "Tusker" (a local beer brand sponsored by East African Breweries Limited). KCB (sponsored by Kenya Commercial Bank Limited), Posta Rangers (sponsored by Postal Corporation of Kenya) and Kenya Pipeline (sponsored by Kenya Pipeline Company) are some of the sporting clubs sponsored by various companies in the country.

8.4.4.10 Personal selling

Personal selling is also highly utilized in Kenya. In most supermarkets, there are dedicated salespeople for certain product lines or even brands. This makes it easy for customers to get information about the brands at the point of purchase (see below a photo taken by one of the authors of a Jack Daniels salesperson who was promoting a Jack Daniels sauce in a liquor store in Nairobi). As is evident, the sales pitch was happening at the point of purchase and customers got a free shirt with the purchase of the barbecue sauce (Figures 8.13 and 8.14).

Figure 8.13 Point of Purchase Personal Selling – Jack Daniel's.
Source: Photo by author.

8.4.4.11 Sales Promotions

Many companies utilize different sales promotion tools. Most supermarkets have customer loyalty programs designed to tie the customer to the specific retailer. Carrefour, one of the largest supermarkets, has a loyalty program known as "MyClub", while Chandarana, another important grocery store, has a loyalty

Figure 8.14 Promotional T-Shirt and Barbecue Give Aways: Ja k Daniel's.

Source: Photo by author.

card. These loyalty programs seek to tie the consumer to the retailer by re-warding the customer with points that are only redeemable with the retailer. Some companies also run competitions and sweepstakes to encourage brand purchases. The photos below show the Chandarana loyalty program and Carrefour's loyalty card.

Figure 8.15 Chandarana Loyalty Program.

Source: Photo by author.

The photos below show the Chandarana loyalty program and Carrefour's loyalty card (Figures 8.15 and 8.16).

Coupons are also a viable way of marketing in Kenya and are utilized by many companies.

See for example the promotion by Carrefour around Ramadhan (Figure 8.17).

8.4.4.12 Market Research

Marketing research is gathering, recording, and analyzing data to provide information useful to marketing decision-making. Generally, the marketing research process is the same whether in Germany or Kenya. Nonetheless, international marketing research involves two additional complications: (1) information must be communicated across cultural boundaries. The translation is critical so that the research idea in one country is understood in the other, and (2) the environments within which the research tools are applied are often different in foreign markets. Market research in foreign markets is much broader in scope due to the existence of higher levels of uncertainty. Generally, foreign business research requires the collection of (1) economic and demographic data; (2) cultural, sociological, and political climate data; (3) an overview of market conditions; (4) overview of the technological environment and (5) review of the competitive situation. Gathering all this information is necessary for a company to become intimate with the environment, the dynamics of the market, and customer behavior. To build suitable marketing strategies, marketers must have good

Figure 8.16 Carrefour MyClub Loyalty Program.

Source: Photo by author.

Figure 8.17 Carrefour Ramadan Coupon.

Source: Photo by author.

and workable data that will measure the variables that are needed to do the projections and decision-making that is necessary (Cateora et al., 2013).

In the past, face-to-face interviews and surveys were some of the most common ways of data collection in most parts of Africa, including Kenya.

Because of the Covid-19 pandemic, many market research companies created virtual data collection methods. Research informants also became more comfortable with virtual data collection methods, which has changed how research is conducted in many regions of the world, including Kenya. Several reputable market research companies in Kenya offer both primary and secondary research services. Often, these firms can conduct qualitative or quantitative research studies based on the needs of their clients.

8.4.4.13 Primary Research

The main data collection methods that Kenyan market research companies utilize are household interviews, email and online panels, street intercepts, online questionnaires, computer-aided telephone interviews, mobile-assisted personal interviews, mystery shopping, etc. Additionally, some companies offer qualitative research methods such as focus groups, in-depth interviews, key informant interviews, observations, ethnography, etc. Some key market research companies include Research 8020, Consumer Insight, Survey and Statistics Solutions Kenya, Consumer Options Ltd., Infinite Sight Ltd., Research Solution Africa Ltd., and many others (Kamau, 2021).

It is important to note that all persons intending to undertake research in Kenya must obtain a research permit. The National Commission for Science, Technology, and Innovation (NACOSTI) can obtain the research permit. The application guidelines and fees can be found on the NACOSTI research portal (https://research-portal.nacosti.go.ke/).

8.5 Marketing Strategies

Marketing research enables a company to formulate marketing strategies that will generate superior returns for stakeholders and result in satisfied customers. The manipulation of the marketing mix represents the essence of a company's marketing strategy. It is a set of strategic decisions about the company's products and their promotion, pricing, and distribution activities to meet the consumers' needs in their target markets. The company can standardize or adapt its marketing strategies depending on the market, the consumer needs and the demographic characteristics of the respective markets. The standardized approach is much easier due to the benefits of economies of scale and is undoubtedly less expensive. A standardized approach enables the company to implement marketing strategies that already exist. As demonstrated, a company doing business in Kenya must customize its marketing strategies by adapting some marketing mix variables. This is more expensive than selling a product in a standard way, but adaptation will result in products ideal for the target market in Kenya. The previous sections highlighted examples of companies that have successfully modified their strategies through such tactics as developing small-sized products, lower-priced products, motorcycle delivery of products, promotion of products on radio, and sponsorship of YouTube talk shows, etc. Kenya is a diversified and geographically different market, and as Geringer et al. (2020) noted, different geographic and cultural areas have different customer needs, which require different marketing mix approaches. Therefore, companies doing business in Kenya must adapt their marketing strategies to suit the reality of the Kenyan consumer and market.

8.6 Discussion

Consumers around the world are highly demanding and knowledgeable. The competitive conditions surrounding businesses in Kenya require them to respond with properly designed marketing strategies. Enterprises must be innovative, invest in technology, and meet the challenges of constant changes in the competitive environment. Effective marketing strategies ensure that a company satisfies its customers and increases customer value. The consequence of these actions allows companies to understand customer needs and enhance company performance. Marketing strategies have a great influence on performance. The level of adaptation of each marketing strategy component can positively influence a firm's performance.

8.7 Conclusion

This chapter has provided the reader with general definitions of marketing and the marketing process. The authors sought to highlight some key considerations for successful marketing in Kenya. Marketing is about the exchange, and all marketing activities are designed to facilitate exchange. In this chapter, the authors have shown that exchange will happen in Kenya just like in other parts of the world, and they have provided a roadmap for marketing in Kenya. After reading this chapter, we hope the reader feels prepared to market in Kenya.

References

American Marketing Association Definition (2017). https://www.ama.org/the-definition-of-marketing-what-is-marketing/, accessed April 5, 2022.
Alliance Media. https://www.alliancemedia.com/ accessed, April 25 2022.
Barassa, N. Personal communication, January 12, 2022. Nairobi Kenya.
Bhushan, R. and Pande, B. (2010). Rs 5 price point becomes a magic word for marketers across products, ET Bureau December 4th https://economictimes.indiatimes.com/industry/services/advertising/rs-5-price-point-becomes-a-magic-word-for-marketers-acrossproducts/articleshow/7154300.cms?from=mdr, accessed on March 28, 2022.
Boyo, C. (2021). Media Personality Jalang'o: I have never ever stolen from anyone, The Nairobian, September 3, 2021, https://www.standardmedia.co.ke/thenairobian/entertainment/2001422526/comedian-jalango-i-am-an-influencer-for-1001-brands, accessed April 5, 2022.

Business Daily (2021). YouTube content creators to get Shs.1 million monthly, https://www.businessdailyafrica.com/bd/corporate/technology/youtube-content-creators-get-sh1m-monthly-3533918, accessed April 5, 2022.

Chege, J. Personal communication, December 2021, Jason Chege (CEO), https://cafengoma.co.ke/#the-agency

Cateora, G. and Graham (2013). *International Marketing*, 16th edition, New York: McGraw-Hill.

Cateora, P.R., Money, R.B., Gilly, M.C. and Graham, J.L. (2020). *International Marketing*, 18th edition, Dubuque: McGraw-Hill Education.

Competition Authority of Kenya (2022). Our functions. Retrieved from m https://cak.go.ke/enforcement-and-compliance, accessed May 5, 2022.

Country Commerical Guide (2021). Kenya – Country commercial guide, https://www.trade.gov/country-commercial-guides/kenya-selling-factors-and-techniques

Croft, R., Dean, D., and Kitchen, P. (1996). Word-of-mouth communication: Breath of life or kiss of death? In: The Proceedings of the Marketing Education Group Conference, Glasgow: The Department of Marketing, University of Strathclyde.

Daily Nation, National Publications Limited (NPL) rate card https://www.mwnation.com/rate-card/, accessed April 5, 2022.

Defining International Marketing 6.4 (NA) in Business Fundamentals https://cnx.org/contents/1ttgPM0x@4.3NH6_z7EQ/Defining-international-marketing, accessed August 17, 2021.

Dijkstra, T., Meulenberg, M., and Tilburg, A. v. (2001). Applying marketing channel theory to food marketing in developing countries: Vertical disintegration model for horticultural marketing channels in Kenya, *Agribusiness*, 17(2), 227–241.

Empire Group. https://theempire.com/tv-advertising/kenya/, accessed April 5, 2022.

Erdogan, B.Z. (1999). Celebrity endorsement: A literature review, *Journal of Marketing Management*, 15, 291–314.

Geringer, M., McNett, J.M., and Ball, D. (2020). *International Business*, 2nd edition, New York: McGraw – Hill.

Gitonga, S. (2020). Top digital influencers in Kenya, Business Today, April 14, 2020, https://businesstoday.co.ke/digital-influencers-in-kenya-top-digital-influencers-in-kenya-top-digital-influencers-in-kenya/, accessed April 4, 2022.

Kamau, S. (2021), List of market research companies, firms available in Kenya, June 01, 2021. https://www.tuko.co.ke/269593-list-market-research-companies-kenya.html, accessed April 5, 2022.

KBC (2022). M-pesa-announces-kshs-20-million-sponsorship-ahead-of-magical-kenya-ladies-open, https://www.kbc.co.ke/m-pesa-announces-kshs-20-million-sponsorship-ahead-of-magical-kenya-ladies-open/, accessed April 4, 2022.

Kenya Bureau of Standards. https://www.kebs.org/, accessed on April 5, 2022.

Kenyan street vendors. https://kenasvit.wordpress.com/about-kenasvit/, accessed April 5, 2022.

Kenya Film Classification Board, https://kfcb.go.ke/, accessed April 5, 2022.

Kenya Revenue Authority. https://www.kra.go.ke/individual/filing-paying/types-of-taxes/value-added-tax, accessed on April 5, 2022.

Kimani, E.W., Gachigua, S.G., and Kariuki, G.M. (2020). Locked-in metaphorically: The war on Hawking in Nairobi's CBD and the cat-and-mouse game, Africa Development, Volume XLV, No. 4, 2020, pp. 157–182 © Council for the Development of Social Science Research in Africa, 2021 (ISSN: 0850 3907) https://www.jstor.org/stable/10.2307/27008616

Kohli, A.K. and Jaworski, B. (1990). Market orientation: The construct, research propositions, and managerial implications, *Journal of Marketing*, April, 54(2), 1–18. DOI: 10.1177/002224299005400201.

Lim, O., Salahuddin, R., and Abdullah (2016). Factors influencing online shopping behavior: The mediating role of purchase intention, *Procedia Economics and Finance*, 35, 401–410.

Loyalty Card. https://www.carrefour.ke/mafken/en/, accessed April 5, 2022.

Mang'era, R., Munga, J., and Mbebe, J. (2019). Internet marketing strategies and profitability of retail industry in Kenya, *International Academic Journal of Innovation Leadership and Entrepreneurship*, 2(2), pp. 118–128.

Mastercard Press Release (2021). 79% of Kenyan consumers are shopping more online since the start of pandemic, February 2nd, https://newsroom.mastercard.com/mea/press-releases/79-of-kenyan-consumers-are-shopping-more-online-since-the-start-of-pandemic-reveals-mastercard-study/, accessed April 2, 2022.

Mathew, P.M. and Mishra, S. (2014). Online retailing in India. Linking internet usage perceived risk website attributes and past online purchase behavior, *Electronic Journal of Information Systems in Developing Countries*, 65(1), 1–17.

Mbego, S. (2019). The stats behind our reliance on 'kadogo' buys "*The Standard Newspaper*, https://www.standardmedia.co.ke/business/enterprise/article/2001335115/the-stats-behind-our-reliance-on-kadogo-buys, accessed on April 5, 2022.

MCarthy, J. (1960). Basic Marketing: A managerial approach, Homewood IL: Richard C. Irwin 1 Inc. as cited by Walter van Waterschoot and Christophe Van den Bulte, "The 4P classification of the marketing mix revisited, *Journal of Marketing*, 56, October 1992, 83–93.

McNamara, C.P. (1972). The present status of the marketing concept, *Journal of Marketing*, 36 (January), 50–57.

Media Council of Kenya. https://mediacouncil.or.ke/, accessed April 5, 2022.

Mutuiri, B. (2022). This is what you require to sponsor a sport in Kenya, March 19, 2022. https://www.teamkenya.co.ke/news/3030-what-you-require-sponsor-sport-kenya, accessed on April 1, 2022.

National Commission for Science Technology and Innovation (NACOSTI) https://research-portal.nacosti.go.ke/, accessed on April 1, 2022.

Ngala, L. (2022). ABSA pump KShs. 56 million into Magical Kenya Open, Daily Nation, February 18, 2022, https://nation.africa/kenya/sports/golf/absa-pump-sh56-million-to-magical-kenya-open-3721630, accessed April 4, 2022.

Otieno, D. (2021). Kenya leads the world in WhatsApp Usage, https://tech-ish.com/2021/07/22/kenya-whatsapp-usage-facebook-ajua/, accessed October 30th, 2022.

Otieno, V. (2022). CS Amina approves tax rebates for companies supporting sports, https://nation.africa/kenya/sports/other-sports/cs-amina-approves-tax-rebates-for-companies-supporting-sports-3744812, accessed April 4, 2022.

Paul, J. and Rosenbaum, M.S. (2019). Retailing and consumer services at a tipping point: New conceptual frameworks and theoretical models, *Journal of Retailing and Consumer Services*, 54(7), 101977, DOI: 10.1016/j.jretconser.2019.101977.

Statistica (2022). https://www.statista.com/statistics/889858/radio-advertising-revenue-kenya/, accessed April 5, 2022.

Top marketing agencies in Kenya. https://soravjain.com/digital-marketing-agencies-kenya/, accessed April 5, 2022.

U.S. Commerce Service (2012). Doing business in Kenya: 2012 Country Commercial Guide for U.S. Companies.

UNESCO (2021). UNESCO launches Social Media for Peace project in Kenya https://en.unesco.org/news/unesco-launches-social-media-peace-project-kenya accessed April 5, 2022.

World Population Review. (2021). https://worldpopulationreview.com/country-rankings/facebook-users-by-country, accessed April 5, 2022.

9 Future Trends and Conclusions

9.1 Overview

Chapter 1 presents an overview of Kenya's location, its regional positioning, its business operations and opportunities and its investment climate. Kenya is an East African country with one of the fastest-growing economies in the region.

Chapter 2 analyzes Kenya's business environment and the regional and global factors that define Kenya's investment climate. Kenya's business environment has a robust economy and a formidable competitive position. The authors discuss factors that bolster Kenya's strong investment climate, the country's world and regional positioning, and specific sectors and industries that present business opportunities.

Chapter 3 presents a historical account of Kenya's economic performance from the pre-colonial era to date. Understanding of economic, social and political landscapes and determining patterns and outcomes of events in the past helps to address key questions about current economic developments. We also provide an in-depth analysis of Kenya's legal framework, particularly as it relates to business activity. Kenya's legal system is based on the British common-law tradition, blended with Islamic and customary law, and its judicial system is robust. The chapter also focuses on the types of business ventures in Kenya, including sole proprietorships, partnerships, companies (both domestic and foreign), cooperative societies, and parastatals (state-owned corporations) and how they are created. Every business needs financing to conduct its operations, and we discuss the different sources of finance available in Kenya, including debt and equity.

In Chapter 4 we note that hospitable, stable governments can encourage business investment and growth. Even if a country has abundant valuable natural resources, it becomes undesirable for business when political unrest prevails. Issues of business nationalization, expropriation, and insecurity emerge as negative in the eyes of business investors. Even if a country is endowed with abundant factors of production, an adverse political environment may undermine investment. Political instability significantly increases the risk quotient toward discouraging any business investment.

DOI: 10.4324/9781003095156-9

Chapter 5 discusses Kenya's economic system, which is imperative for attracting investments and doing business. The chapter also highlights Kenya's key economic characteristics, such as gross domestic product, inflation and unemployment, population demographics, and monetary and fiscal policies. Kenya's financial system, consisting of banking, capital markets, insurance pension, savings and credit societies (SACCOs), and digital economy, is also presented in this chapter. We note that investors are interested in these economic metrics as they constitute key attributes of the investment climate. This is an important aspect of the investment process that needs to be understood to make informed choices.

Chapter 6 focuses on culture as a major factor in any business development. Both domestic business entrepreneurship and foreign direct investment (FDI) rely on an accurate understanding of how national cultures and subcultures affect the operation of a business in a country. This chapter focuses on the aspects of culture deemed important in Kenya, especially those that impact business conduct. Explanations of how culture affects business development are at the core of this chapter's discussion. Therefore, the role of language, national culture and subcultures, religion, and interpersonal communication are discussed in detail. Kenyan business customs and etiquette are also discussed.

Chapter 7 provides a detailed methodology for developing a business in Kenya. It delves into the steps necessary to initiate a business and the resources and institutions available during the business development process. Kenya's basic infrastructure and supply chain management is also discussed as well as the importance of corporate social responsibility and its actualization. In addition, a brief description of insurance is presented. The chapter deliberates on the pros and cons of business development in Kenya.

Chapter 8 examines marketing in a Kenyan cultural context. Understanding how marketing is done in Kenya is critical to appreciating how business is transacted in Kenya. A detailed analysis of the Kenyan marketing environment is developed. Marketing strategies that would be suitable and effective in Kenyan business ventures are discussed. This chapter also briefly discusses market research options in Kenya. The adaptation of the marketing mix in Kenya is thoroughly discussed, with particular emphasis on product adaptation, promotion and marketing communication.

9.2 Global Investment Trends

Post-COVID-19 pandemic global performance is bullish with FDI flows rebounding in 2021. FDI is up 77 percent to an estimated $1.65 trillion from $929 billion in 2020 (UNCTAD, 2022). Notable growth is evident in infrastructure finance due to recovery stimulus packages, but greenfield investment activities remain weak across industrial sectors. Developed economies reported the biggest FDI rise by far, representing almost three-quarters of the total global FDI inflows. UNCTAD forecasts a growth trajectory for FDI into Africa, against the backdrop of a lackluster turnaround in the economies, and the COVID pandemic, which is expected to impede the scale of investment recovery. The United States continues to dominate the world as the top destination of FDI. China is the largest recipient of capital investment in Asia-Pacific. Western Europe is the leading source region, accounting for 49 percent of FDI projects globally. Overall, FDI to the African continent was projected to grow by only 5 percent, which is lower than the global and developing countries' forecast growth rates. In East Africa, Ethiopia is the leading recipient of FDI, accounting for more than one-third of foreign investment in the region. It is not clear how the global economy will perform in 2022. The current Russia-Ukraine conflict is likely to negatively impact the global economy– oil and gas prices have risen significantly, resulting in inflation and subdued demand.

On the other hand, the expected rise in demand for commodities will result in higher resource-seeking investments. New opportunities in Africa are expected to open due to the reconfiguration of global value chains and the increasing importance of regional value chains. Moreover,, the impending finalization of the African Continental Free Trade Area (AfCFTA) agreement's Sustainable Investment Protocol could give impetus to intra-continental investment (UNCTAD, 2022). As noted elsewhere, the Kenya Investment Authority KenInvest) is a government agency that promotes and facilitates investment in Kenya. In an interview with one of the authors at their Nairobi offices, KenInvest Managing Director Olivia Rachier, stated that the KenInvest operates under the direction of the board of directors and management team to make Kenya the investment destination of choice. KenInvest's General Manager for Investment Promotion, Pius Rotich, noted that *"Kenya is bigger than Kenya"*. Investors in Kenya have ample access to the entire continent of Africa, with a population of about 1.6 billion, by virtue of the continental and regional integration blocs of the African Continental Free Trade Area (AFCFTA), the Common Market of Eastern and Southern Africa (COMESA), and East African Community (EAC). Kenya also presents a unique strategic geographic location, efficient financial services, modern transport and communication, well skilled human capital, a friendly business climate, and vibrant private sector. According to Garachi Adi, KenInvest's General Manger for Investor Services, investment opportunities abound in *"agricultural value addition, affordable housing appropriate technologies, exports to the USA under the auspices of the African Growth Opportunity Act (AGOA), oil and gas, construction, manufacturing and tourism"* (KenInvest, 2022b) However, Kenya will need reduce the cost of doing business and streamline policies that deter investments.

9.3 Education Trends in Kenya

The population of Kenya is projected to surpass 100 million people by the end of 2058 and reach 125 million by the end of the century (World Population Review, 2021). This increase will significantly expand Kenya's domestic market. Under Vision 2030, the Kenyan government intends to have secured 100 percent literacy rates. Under this vision, primary school education is free with an intended 100 percent transition rate to high schools.

Furthermore, tertiary education is currently being supported with government grants and scholarships (bursaries) to ensure that anybody interested in higher education can access tertiary education institutions. Recently, the government has revamped the education system by introducing the Competency Based Curriculum (CBC). This curriculum prepares Kenyan learners for the new worldwide economic realities. The CBC curriculum is designed to seek out the skills and competencies of different types of learners to result in a learned population, allowing individuals to use their skills to better their own lives and the society at large. The CBC will provide more diverse training, resulting in higher competencies and wages for workers with skills-intense companies (Standard Media). In March 2022, Professor George Magoha, the Cabinet Secretary for Education, said, 'The Competency-Based Curriculum will not be scrapped. CBC is in its seventh year and in a few weeks will be in the eighth year as Grade 6 prepares for Grade 7.' Magoha noted that the CBC was steering learners away from exam-oriented learning and equipping them with skills that would enable them to prosper in the future (Ombima, 2022). According to Chris Diaz, Director EABC and Trustee Brand Africa, economists have argued that education is a major distinguisher between developed and developing economies around the world, with highly competent workers being able to take up opportunities in new and emerging industries such as science and technology (Diaz, C., 2021). The private sector is very interested in how the new CBC will provide a ready workforce for the country.

9.4 Rural Urban Migration

The COVID pandemic resulted in an urban-to-rural shift due to unemployment and the recognition that life in the rural areas was higher quality than in the cities. Nonetheless, as the pandemic continues to recede into our distant memories, it is expected that Kenyans, particularly young Kenyans, will continue to flock to the larger cities in search of higher education and employment opportunities.

9.5 New Business Opportunities

In this section, we discuss available opportunities in Kenya, including real estate, agriculture, manufacturing, financial services, tourism and ICT. The 'new' opportunities comprise mainly innovations on, and expansions of, the traditional business types.

9.5.1 Real Estate

Real estate offers attractive investment opportunities in Kenya, with housing as a backbone sector, contributing to the gross domestic product estimated at 8.5 percent (Center for Affordable Housing Finance in Africa, 2020). Kenya is a populous and growing country with close to 50 million people and a rapidly rising middle-income population. Furthermore, blossoming urbanization has stretched the demand for additional housing in major cities such as Nairobi, Mombasa, and Kisumu. Kenya's annual housing demand is about 250,000 units with an estimated supply of only 50,000 units, resulting in an 80 percent deficit (International Finance Corporation, 2021). About 6.4 million people live in informal settlements, or 12.8 percent of Kenya's urban population. Through Kenya's Affordable Housing Program, a part of its Big 4 Agenda, the government plans to support the construction of 500,000 homes in the next five years (Center for Affordable Housing Finance in Africa, 2020).

The government provides various incentives to the construction sector, such as lowering the corporate tax rate to 15 percent, capping import levies and providing VAT exemptions for inputs, among others. Investors can find an advantage in this sector by offering various services related to project development, including financing, design and master planning, alternative building technologies and energy-efficient structures.

Although financial access has improved, having expanded to over 86 percent in 2020, the mortgage remains a big challenge in the real estate sector. Kenyan banks and builders have historically had difficulties meeting the demand for mortgage products. However, there appears to be increased interest in Kenya's construction sector from the private sector, and multilateral, and bilateral agencies such as IFC, AfDB, and the Chinese Belt and Road Initiative. This is demonstrated by the International Finance Corporation and the African Development Bank collaborating with private and state investors to create the Kenyan Mortgage Refinance Company (KMRC), which provides mortgages to home buyers (International Finance Corporation, 2021). KMRC can now offer fixed-rate term mortgages with long-term maturities for people with modest incomes through its retail mortgage partners. Real estate continues to dominate investment opportunities in Kenya.

Traditionally, investment in real estate has always been a sure bet. The entrance of Chinese, Ethiopian and Indian investors has changed the face of real estate. Many companies are offering real estate products. Optiven is one of the largest real estate companies, and Mr. George Wachiuri founded it. Optiven is a dominant force in the region. It has many flourishing Strategic Business Units (SBUs), including Optiven Real Estate, Optiven Construction, Optiven Insurance, Optiven Homes and Optiven Water.

To learn more about the real estate market in Kenya, the authors interviewed Mr. Wilfred Mose, managing director of the Ruby Group.

Mr. Mose informed the authors that the Ruby group differentiates itself from its competitors by how quickly and efficiently the Ruby group can bring a design concept from idea to development (Mose, 2022). This is because the Ruby Group is a design and build consortium offering a range of real estate services (Rubygroup website). The company has existed for eight years, and they have been involved in projects all over Kenya. Many other important real estate companies in Kenya have operated in this market for over 25 years. Among them are AMG realtors, Hass Consult, Lloyd Masika, Cytonn Real Estate, and Azizi Realtors. The Construction Authority of Kenya regulates the real estate market.

9.5.2 Wholesale and Retail Trade

The wholesale and retail trade sector contributes significantly to Kenya's GDP. According to a local news company, the retail sector is the fifth largest contributor in sub-Saharan Africa and the third biggest contributor to the private sector industry. Real opportunities for foreign investors lie here. Recently, Carrefour solidified its imprint in Kenya and is on course to become the largest retail and supermarket chain in the country. This comes after a short tenure in the country. Consistent with other regions in the world, online retailing will continue to be a key method of selling goods, especially as the infrastructure continues to be developed. Social media and other digital forms of promotion will continue to play a critical role in advertising products on these e-commerce platforms. Jumia.co.ke, Priceinkenya, Phoneplacekenya.com, Shopit.co.ke, and other online retailers will continue to grow in popularity.

9.5.3 Agriculture

Agriculture is the major driving force of economic growth in Kenya, accounting for about 33 percent of the economy's total value. Major agricultural activities include tea, coffee, floriculture and horticulture farming (KenIvest 2022). Investment opportunities in this sector are improving crop yields, processing and storage facilities, agri-business, and marketing and distribution services. There is a push for young people to enter the agricultural space and to incorporate technology into farming. Some of the best agribusiness ideas are dairy farming, hass avocado farming, beekeeping, pig farming, fertilizer distribution, vegetable farming, fresh juice processing, and tree tomato farming, among others (Obiero, 2020).

9.5.4 Tourism

Kenya is a leading tourist destination in Africa. Major tourist attractions are spectacular fauna and flora, wildlife, safari parks, water-based tourism, cultural tourism, and others (KenIvest, 2022). Domestic tourism, particularly during festive seasons, is fast growing in Kenya. The country is home to approximately 50 million people with over 40 tribes and cultures, attracting tourists. During the COVID-19 pandemic, the Kenyan government, through the ministry of tourism, launched the 'Tembea Tujenge Kenya' initiative. The campaign was aimed at boosting the growth of domestic tourism in Kenya by encouraging more local travel as the hotel sector continued to recover from the effects of the pandemic. Maina Kageni is an important brand ambassador of the initiative whose focus, he said, was on marketing campaigns and initiatives aimed at attracting Kenyans to take up domestic tourism to contribute to national priorities such as economic growth, job creation and poverty alleviation (Capital FM, 2022). The campaign, sponsored by the Tourism Fund, Safaricom, Isuzu East Africa, Shell/Vivo energy, Sarova Hotels, St. John's Ambulance and BT Concepts, will continue until 2024.

The Kenyan government has made policies geared toward elevating Kenya's attractiveness to the world's top ten tourist destinations by improving security and providing incentives for investing in the tourism industry. Investment opportunities abound in tourist services in Kenya. Kenya has beautiful beaches and excellent golf courses. At 2020, World Golf Awards Gala Ceremony, Kenya's Karen Country Club won the best golf course in Africa (Ngala, 2020, Daily Nation).

9.5.5 Finance and Financial Services

As discussed in Chapter 3, Kenya has developed advanced financial systems and services compared to other sub-Saharan countries. The increased adoption of technology and a stable regulatory environment have contributed to the growth of Kenya's financial sector. This sector provides many investment opportunities in Kenya. With the increased number of young people utilizing mobile phones and the internet, and with Kenyans' overall comfort of using mobile payment systems such as M-Pesa, Kenyans seem poised to take full advantage of cryptocurrency and blockchain innovations. Many young Kenyan business professionals are championing the adoption of cryptocurrency. For example, John Wainaina Karanja, the CEO, and Co-founder of Melanin Solar has been pushing the adoption of cryptocurrency across the African continent through Melanin Solar's subsidiary BitHub Africa. Michal Kimani, a Kenyan businessman, is Africa's number one crypto and blockchain operator. Additionally, Kimani trains and consults with company leaders on creating or investing in the African crypto and blockchain market (Remitano, 2021).

9.5.6 Manufacturing

Manufacturing is one key sector in Kenya's Big 4 Agenda development program. Business opportunities in this sector are food processing, textile and steel (KenIvest, 2022). The government provides incentives and a friendly regulatory regime in this sector. One of the authors visited Kitui County Textile Center (KICOTEC), a manufacturing plant in Kitui that is part of a development initiative by Charity Ngilu, the governor of Kitui. KICOTEC was the first garment factory set up by a county in the devolved counties to address unemployment. Currently, KICOTEC manufactures uniforms for government officers, such as chiefs, and employs more than 300 people (KICOTEC Website).

9.5.7 Information and Communication Technology

Kenya is a regional leader in terms of broadband connectivity, and communication technology (ICT) infrastructure, value-added services, mobile money, and mobile banking services (KenIvest, 2022). The country's ICT sector is set to account for up to 8 percent of the country's GDP. Internet access has continued to spur economic growth, which contributed to the government's development of a framework to improve Kenya's ability to spur economic growth in the region.

The COVID-19 pandemic has significantly accelerated digitalization and opened new opportunities for telecom operators, hardware and software vendors. According to the Economist Intelligence Unit (EIU), fast, reliable connections have become vital to businesses, consumers, and governments as they try to cope with the global crisis. For businesses, the pandemic has underlined the benefits of online offerings, automation, and the development of the Internet of Things (IoT) to manage supply chains. For consumers, it has increased demand for online goods and services. In contrast, governments it has highlighted the importance of deploying online services, including healthcare, and the potential benefits of advanced data analytics, artificial intelligence (AI) and robotics.

In Kenya, all 47 counties have ICT Roadmaps aligned with the National ICT Master plan and local county development plans (CDPs). Through roadmaps, counties can provide their citizens the best cost-effective ICT-enabled services and resources. The ICT roadmaps have also helped county governments make ICT investments consistent with global best practices. Additionally, neighboring counties have recognized the need to collaborate on ICT infrastructure development with the central government to secure superior services for their citizens.

For Kenya to meet the critical ICT workforce needs and skills gap, the ICT Authority, in collaboration with other ICT stakeholders, has developed various skills and programs to manage the challenge of the gap between industry talent needs (ICT Authority, 2022). The Authority has also partnered with leading U.S. companies such as Oracle and Microsoft for skills development and programs, including the E-government capacity building program and ICT skills training.

A continued push by the government to provide more of its services online has contributed to the demand-driven growth of the sector. Some of the automated government services include online applications for acquiring a Personal Identification Number (PIN) for tax purposes and the introduction of iTax, a platform where citizens can file their annual tax returns online.

Kenya is currently one of Africa's fastest-growing ICT markets; companies have increased productivity in all spheres of the production process and enabled an expansion of skills. Investment opportunities in this sector include hardware and software products, support services, and call centers.

9.6 Implications and Next Steps

The Kenyan government has historically supported business, which will continue. Kenya is a member of the East African Community (EAC) comprises Kenya, Uganda, Burundi, Rwanda, Tanzania and the Democratic Republic of the Congo (DRC), which joined the EAC in April 2022. This edition of the DRC means that companies in Kenya will now have access to an expanded market of 300 million consumers. Kenya remains an excellent country in which to start a business and continues to attract many investors. In April 2022, Dr. Fisk Johnson, CEO of SC Johnson, visited Kenya and shared his company's intent to resume purchasing pyrethrum from Kenya as SC Johnson continues to produce chemicals to fight malaria (Wanjiru, 2022). In April 2022, Google announced its plans to open a product development center in Nairobi. The Google center will build 'transformative' products and services for the African market and the world (Daily Nation, 2022). Earlier in April, Microsoft launched a research and development center in Nairobi.

Meanwhile, Visa announced that it had set up its first innovation hub to co-create payment and commerce solutions with partners (Daily Nation, 2022). It is noteworthy that these global companies continue to invest in Kenya because of its excellent potential and track record for business success. Kenya is open for investment despite some persistent challenges such as corruption. The government continues to work on reducing corruption, and recent transparency international rankings show that Kenya is on the right trajectory concerning corruption reduction. Currently, the country ranks 128/180 (2022), 124/180 (2021), 137/180 (2019), and 144/180 (2018) (Transparency International, 2022).

Other areas that could benefit from improvement are government efficiencies and the pace of starting a business in Kenya. While the number of days needed to start a business has greatly decreased, it is still evident that there are inefficiencies when starting a business in Kenya. The government continues to work on 'ease of doing business,' and this has resulted in Kenya improving its ease of doing business from 61 in 2018 to 56 in 2019.

9.7 Conclusion

In conclusion, Kenya offers many business opportunities. It is ripe for investment. It has a youthful population and rising middle-class consumers.

Kenyans speak English and, in general, value and appreciate Western brands. Investing in Kenya is an important choice for any company or individual looking to invest in Africa. This book has provided a roadmap for potential investors in Kenya. We have highlighted important aspects of the political, economic, social, technological, environmental, legal (PESTEL), and cultural environment.

Additionally, we have examined how the marketing mix variables can be adopted in Kenya. Information about available resources and facilitating organizations have also been presented. The authors hope this information gives future investors an adequate roadmap for investing in Kenya. Karibuni Kenya (Welcome to Kenya).

References

Capital FM (2022). Shows. https://radio.capitalfm.co.ke/, accessed April 15th, 2022.

Center for Affordable Housing Finance in Africa (2020). Africa Housing Finance Yearbook 2020: Kenya. https://housingfinanceafrica.org/app/uploads/V13-Kenya.pdf, accessed June 24th 2022.

Diaz, C. (2021). New curriculum can re-engineer the workplace, economy, *The Sunday Standard*, February 16th. Accessed at https://www.standardmedia.co.ke/commentary/article/2001403626/new-curriculum-can-re-engineer-the-workplace-economy, on April 24, 2022.

ICT Authority (2022). Projects. https://icta.go.ke/contact-us, accessed June 24th, 2022.

International Finance Corporation (2021). A Kenyan Home of One's Own. https://www.ifc.org/wps/wcm/connect/news_ext_content/ifc_external_corporate_site/news+and+events/news/affordable-housing-kenya, accessed June 24th 2022.

KenInvest (2022a). E-Opportunities. http://www.invest.go.ke/why-invest-in-kenya/#, accessed June 24th, 2022.

KenInvest (2022b). Personal communication, Olivia Rachier, Pius Rotich, Garachi Adi, at KenInvest Offices Nairobi Kenya, January 13th, 2022.

KICOTEC Website. Kitui County Textile Center, http://www.invest.go.ke/https://kitui.go.ke/countygovt/works/kicotec-kitui-county-textile-center/, accessed April 24th, 2022.

Kimuyu, H. (2022). Google opens product development center in Nairobi, its first in Africa, *Daily Nation*, April 20th 2022, https://nation.africa/kenya/news/google-opens-product-development-centre-in-nairobi its first-in-africa-3788318, accessed April 24th, 2022.

Mose, W. (2022). Personal communication by Zoom Interview - March 12 2022. Ruby Group Website, https://rubygroup.co.ke/home/, accessed April 25th, 2022.

Ngala, L. (2020). Kenya Ranked as Africa's Best Golfing Destination. https://allafrica.com/stories/202011030166.html, accessed April 22nd, 2022.

Obiero, G.M. (2020). 15 profitable agribusiness ideas in Kenya 2020 published June 24th, 2020, *Tuko*. Accessed at https://www.tuko.co.ke/262733-agribusiness-ideas-kenya-2020.html, accessed April 24th, 2022.

Ombima, M. (2022). The CBC is here to stay, *The Star*, February 24th 2022 https://www.the-star.co.ke/counties/western/2022-02-24-cbc-here-to-stay-says-magoha/, accessed April 24th 2022.

Remitano (2021). Top 10 Crypto Influencers in Africa to Follow in 2021, https://remitano.com/btc/au/post/12602-top-10-crypto-influencers-in-africa-to-follow, accessed April 22nd, 2022.

Transparency International (2022). Corruption Index, https://www.transparency.org/en/cpi/2018/index/ken, accessed April 24th, 2022.

UNCTAD (2022). Global foreign direct investment rebounded strongly in 2021, but the recovery is highly uneven. *UNCTAD*. Retrieved from https://unctad.org/news/global-foreign-direct-investment-rebounded-strongly-2021-recovery-highly-uneven

Wanjiru, M. (2022). Kenya partners with SC Johnson and Sons in malaria fight, *Star*. https://www.the-star.co.ke/news/2022-04-06-kenya-partners-with-sc-johnson-and-sons-in-malaria-fight/, accessed April 24th, 2022.

World Population Review (2021). *World population by countries*. https://worldpopulationreview.com/, accessed October 15th, 2022.

Index

Page numbers followed by f indicate figure

Printed in the United States
by Baker & Taylor Publisher Services